50 Ways to Love Your Woman

Approaching the Heart with a Rational Mind

Sarah Cline, Ph.D.

Copyright © 2023 Sarah Cline, Ph.D.
All rights reserved.

The contents of this book may not be reproduced, duplicated, or transmitted without direct written permission from the author.

Under no circumstances will any legal responsibility or blame be held against the publisher for any reparation, damages, or monetary loss due to the information herein, either directly or indirectly.

Legal Notice:

This book is copyright-protected. This is only for personal use. You cannot amend, distribute, sell, use, quote, or paraphrase any part of the content within this book without the consent of the author.

Disclaimer Notice:

Please note the information contained within this document is for educational and entertainment purposes only. Every attempt has been made to provide accurate, up-to-date, and reliable complete information. No warranties of any kind are expressed or implied. Readers acknowledge that the author is not engaging in the rendering of legal, financial, medical, or professional advice. The content of this book has been derived from various sources. Please consult a licensed professional before attempting any techniques outlined in this book.

By reading this document, the reader agrees that under no circumstances is the author responsible for any losses, direct or indirect, which are incurred as a result of the use of the information contained within this document, including, but not limited to, errors, omissions, or inaccuracies.

ISBN: 978-1-937209-24-7

Contents

Introduction — 1

1. Understanding Your Woman's Personality Type — 4
   Origins of Personality Types
   Cave Dweller (CD) and Mountain Yeller (MY) Women
   The Cave Dweller (CD) Woman
   Deeper Dive into the Mountain Yeller (MY) Woman
   The Straddler Woman
   Key Takeaways

2. Communication Is Key — 21
   Express Feelings Gently Without Starting Conflicts
   Practice Active Listening
   Use Neutral Language to Avoid Escalation
   Appreciate Silence and Peace with CDs
   Offer Verbal Affirmations and Reassurance to MYs
   Understand and Be Mindful of Personal Boundaries
   Engage in Relationship and Emotional Check-ins
   Set Aside Time for Reflection and Understanding
   Embrace Spontaneity and Passion
   Share Personal Growth Moments Regularly
   Key Takeaways

3. Enhance the Intimacy — 39
    Understand Sexual Dynamics Between CDs and MYs
    Build an Emotional Bond with CDs
    Highlight MYs' Need for Physical Closeness
    Offer Surprise Romantic Gestures Catered to Each Type
    Organize Thoughtful Date Nights
    Take a Walk Down Memory Lane
    Discuss Your Sex Life Openly and Honestly
    Surprise Your Partner with Special Gifts or Excursions
    Realize There's More to Intimacy than Sex
    Discuss Desires and Needs Periodically
    Key Takeaways

4. Balancing Social Lives — 59
    Complement CDs' Need for Solitude with MYs' Social Inclinations
    Plan Activities Catered to Each Personality
    Gradually Introduce CDs to Social Settings
    Appreciate MYs' Need for Exciting Social Engagements
    Set Healthy Boundaries
    Engage in Joint Activities, Both In and Outside the Home
    Allow Nights Out with Friends and Loved Ones
    Host or Attend Social Events or Gatherings
    Celebrate Milestones Together
    Acknowledge and Praise Individual Achievements
    Key Takeaways

5. Resonating Emotionally — 59
    Celebrate the Emotional Strengths Each Type Brings to the Partnership
    Offer Support to MYs in their Social Endeavors

Understand and Listen to CDs in their Introspective Moments

Recognize and Validate Each Other's Fears and Vulnerabilities

Explore A Wide Range of Emotions Together Through Media and Art

Key Takeaways

6. Maintaining Healthy Finances 59

    Address Financial Matters with Patience and Understanding

    Make a Financial Plan or Goal Together

    Navigate Familial and External Financial Opinions

    Respect Each Type's Financial Priorities and Plan for Future Securities, Such as Investments and Savings

    Remember That You Two Are a Team Working Toward a Shared Goal

    Key Takeaways:

7. Cultivate a Lifelong Romance 59

    Renew Commitment Vows on Milestone Dates

    Take Time for You and Your Partner to Laugh and Have Fun

    Engage in Romantic Activities Such as Couple Massages or Weekend Getaways

    Don't Be Afraid of Counseling When Needed

    Experience New Activities, Hobbies, or Restaurants Together

    Share and Support Each Other's Dreams and Aspirations

    Respect and Encourage Each Other's Personal Development

Revisit Places of Mutual Significance
  Celebrate Anniversaries with Unique Traditions
  Create and Maintain Relationship Rituals and Promises
  Key Takeaways

8. Final Thoughts — 59
  The Importance of Continuous Effort and Growth in Relationships
  Embrace the Dynamic Nature of Love
  Learn Through Differences
  Cherish Your Love

Appendices — 59
  Self-Assessment Questionnaire: Determine if You're a CD, MY, or Straddler

Introduction

Welcome to *50 Ways to Love Your Woman*. If you've picked up this book, you may be in a challenging relationship, eager to enhance an existing bond, or just gearing up for your future romantic life. Whatever the case, you've taken a significant step toward deeper understanding and connection. Congratulations are in order!

Throughout this volume and larger series, we'll focus on three universal personality categories: the reserved Cave Dweller (CD), the outgoing Mountain Yeller (MY), and the Straddler, who exhibits mixed traits. Recognizing and understanding these types is crucial, as they shape relationship dynamics in untold ways. Our aim is to provide practical insights into fundamental personalities, equipping you with the tools to better navigate and strengthen your relationships. What's more, you'll walk away with a more profound grasp of who *you* truly are because it is through knowing ourselves that we can better understand and empathize with others.

Armed with the insights from this book, you'll not only be able to interpret actions but also understand the deeper motivations behind them with greater ease. Prepare to see your woman—and perhaps yourself—in a whole new light.

The Power of Personalities

In this book, we'll demystify the core attributes of CDs, MYs, and Straddlers, equipping you with insights to comprehend and appreciate the nuances of each type. Appreciating these differences allows you to interpret your woman's behaviors accurately within her unique personality context, thus avoiding flawed assumptions.

Too often in relationships, we mistakenly attribute conflicts and misunderstandings to a lack of love, empathy, or respect. Yet, more frequently, it's a simple gap in understanding. When we don't perceive the underlying personality traits driving our partners' actions, we can misinterpret their intentions, leading to undue tension. It's not always about agreeing or having the same viewpoint; it's about acknowledging and respecting these inherent differences. By recognizing the core personality traits of CDs, MYs, and Straddlers, we can better empathize with our partners, allowing love to flourish fully.

Before We Begin

50 Ways to Love Your Woman is not a quick fix or casual checklist. Instead, it emphasizes "love" as an active endeavor, demanding attention and effort. While you'll find a great deal of guidance here, authentically applying these insights is up to you.

Engaging with this material will require introspection. There will be moments that challenge your current understanding of relationships—and everything else. Yet, it's in these times of reflection and adjustment that true growth happens. Here, the fruits of your labor could scarcely be sweeter.

Through patience and ongoing application, you're not just enhancing a single bond but, rather, refining how you connect—how you live—how you share your soul. So, love the process, love yourself, and love your woman on a whole new level.

Before we begin, remind yourself—you're a masterpiece and a work in progress. You are here to learn, discover, and transform your relationships. Now, let's begin!

Chapter One

Understanding Your Woman's Personality Type

Do you find yourself struggling to understand your female partner's personality traits? Are you frustrated that they're so dissimilar to yours? Chances are, when you first met your woman, you enjoyed the differences she brought to the table. But once the honeymoon period was over, those differences likely became a source of frustration, misunderstanding, and even strife.

Understanding personality types is an essential piece of the puzzle when seeking to understand your woman. Appreciating your partner means discovering their many layers and complexities, and all of them should garner your attention if you're to experience a happy and healthy relationship.

In this chapter, we will discuss the personality types of the Cave Dweller woman, which we will refer to as the CD woman, the Mountain Yeller or MY woman, and the Straddler woman. Learning about these three basic personality types will give you a clearer picture of the unique benefits and challenges each creates. And understanding is an essential first step to bringing harmony and happiness into your everyday life.

Origins of Personality Types

Long before the modern-day classifications of CDs and MYs and even before psychiatrists and psychologists stepped onto the scene, ancient civilizations sought to explain human behavior and its various nuances.

The Ancient Greeks

The ancient Greeks developed the theory of "four humors" to explain the causes of health and illness, both mental and physical. This theory suggested that an individual's temperament was influenced by bodily fluids: blood (sanguine), yellow bile (choleric), black bile (melancholic), and phlegm (phlegmatic). The Greeks thought these humors were directly related to being sanguine (cheerful), choleric (short-tempered), melancholic (reserved), or phlegmatic (relaxed). Therefore, the balance of these humors was believed to influence an individual's temperament, health, and overall disposition. In contrast, an imbalance of these humors led to behaviors that, today, we associate with certain mental illnesses. For example:

- Sanguine (blood) was associated with cheerful, optimistic, enthusiastic personality traits. An imbalance was thought to be due to a person having too much blood in their body, which would cause a person to be overly confident and have impulsive behavior. Possible precursors to narcissistic and/or bipolar disorder.

- Choleric (yellow bile) was associated with being ambitious, passionate, and easily angered. An imbalance causes anger, irritability, highly aggressive behavior, and rage—possible indicators of borderline personality disorder.

- Melancholic (black bile) was associated with being thoughtful, reflective, and often sad or depressed. This imbalance was associated with melancholy and depression.

- Phlegmatic (phlegm) was associated with being calm, reliable, and often unemotional or apathetic. An imbalance was associated with lethargy, sluggishness, or a lack of motivation, which, much like melancholic, is a symptom of depression.

Treating these emotional ailments is where things got even more interesting. If the Greeks thought you had an imbalance of any of these four humors, you would likely have received one of the following treatments:

- **Dietary Changes:** Prescribed depending on the humor in excess. For instance, someone deemed overly choleric might be advised to avoid hot or spicy foods that would "agitate" the yellow bile.

- **Bloodletting:** If you were believed to have an excess of sanguine humor, it was common practice for the Greeks to prescribe bloodletting. This process involved removing blood from the body by way of leeches or actual cutting.

- **Purging:** In order to remove excess bile or phlegm, laxatives were used, as were emetics, which induced vomiting.

- **Baths/Sweating:** To promote toxin removal, balms, and ointments were applied to the skin to help balance any of these four humors.

The Greeks' attempts to "treat" imbalances in personality or health were based on the observations and the knowledge they had at the time. The four humors theory was eventually replaced with more accurate medical models, but its influence can still be seen in some of our languages today.

The Introvert and The Extrovert

Carl Gustav Jung (1875–1961) was a Swiss psychiatrist, psychoanalyst, and the father of analytical psychology. He developed several concepts that had a profound influence on both psychology and popular culture. One of his most notable contributions was the concept of "introversion" and "extraversion" (often used in the more modern manner: introvert and extrovert). Jung's theory asserts that introversion and extraversion are attitudes that represent the direction in which a person's psychic energy flows.

Extraversion (Extrovert)

According to Jung, the extrovert's energy flows outward. This personality type is more oriented toward the external world and derives energy from interacting with its surroundings, including people, events, and situations. If your woman is an extrovert, she tends to be more outgoing, social, and interested in external events. She's typically action-oriented and is more comfortable in social situations than an introverted woman. Many extroverts are highly influenced by external factors and are occasionally prone to negative introspection.

Introversion (Introvert)

As the name suggests, the introvert's energy flows inward. This personality type is more oriented toward her inner world, relying on introspection and internal reflection. If your partner is introverted, she is generally more reserved and often feels more comfortable with individual activities or smaller group settings. She derives energy and pleasure from thinking, daydreaming, or exploring ideas. Although an introverted woman's daily practices tend to lead to social isolation, many have a small number of deep connections with people of their choosing.

Jung believed that everyone has an introverted and extroverted side, with one being more dominant than the other. It's a spectrum, and while some women might be near the extremes of that spectrum, most individuals lie somewhere in between.

Cave Dweller (CD) and Mountain Yeller (MY) Women

While not strictly rooted in these historical contexts, the CD and MY classifications are evolved constructs reflecting the same human desire to understand ourselves and others in our world more deeply.

While our contemporary understanding of the CD and MY classifications doesn't stem directly from ancient Greek or Jungian theories, much like their historical counterparts, they are observed patterns in modern relationships. By identifying recurring patterns, we can forge tools to help us navigate and harmonize our interpersonal interactions.

The Cave Dweller (CD) Woman

To determine whether you and your woman fall into the CD or MY category, we must first learn about their traits.

Reserved Nature

If your woman is a CD, she will predominantly showcase a calm and reserved demeanor. She is introspective and tends to hold her emotions close to her chest because she values her inner world and the sanctuary it provides. Her reserved nature doesn't mean that she is indifferent or doesn't care about her partner; it just means that she processes her emotions internally and over time.

For instance, after an argument, a CD woman might choose to withdraw to process her feelings rather than immediately confront an issue. A CD woman does this because she feels uncomfortable with strife and needs time to work through her emotions and figure out how to communicate her feelings.

Socially, a CD woman is often found in quieter corners, engaging in a deep conversation with one or two individuals rather than in the center of a party. In group discussions, a CD will offer insights only if specifically asked or if she feels strongly about a topic.

Logical Thinking and Literal Communication

A CD woman leans more toward analytical and logical thinking. She makes decisions only after careful contemplation and weighing the pros and cons. She works hard to keep her emotions from clouding her judgment. This logical thinking manifests in her communication; she will get right to the point without inserting emotions or using stories to embellish her point.

For example, if you discuss a film with a CD woman, she will likely dissect plot points with impeccable logic and point out strengths and weaknesses. But she often misses the emotional undertones of the movie. If you ask a CD if she liked the cake you brought for dessert, she might reply, "Yes," without diving into flowery descriptives.

It's important to note that a CD woman may also get frustrated with an embellished story that doesn't immediately get to the point. It doesn't mean she doesn't want to hear the story or doesn't care what the person has to say; her brain is just geared toward immediate outcomes.

Need for Space

A CD woman has an inherent need for both emotional and physical space. For her, requiring personal space is not about distancing herself from loved ones. It's about needing solitude to recharge and reflect.

CD women enjoy reading books in a cozy nook or going for solitary walks. They may listen to music while cooking dinner instead of talking. This alone time is essential for a CD woman, especially after a day filled with social interactions.

Singular Focus

A CD woman has unparalleled concentration when engrossed in a task and prefers completing that task to her satisfaction before tackling another.

If you attempt to talk to a CD woman while she's writing an email, for example, she may be so absorbed in what she's writing that she'll tune you out. It's not that what you're saying is unimportant to her; it's just challenging for her to spread her focus on more than one task at a time because she gives each item her full attention.

Social Preferences

Traditionally, if your woman were labeled an introvert, many would consider her anti-social. But that couldn't be further from the truth. An introvert, or a CD woman, just leans toward more intimate social interactions. Large gatherings can overwhelm a CD woman and quickly drain her mental and emotional battery.

Emotional Processing

While CD women might not outwardly express their emotions, they experience them intensely. However, their internal reflections may lead to a delay in their outward emotional expression. While a CD woman may seem distant after an emotional confrontation, many need to process the interaction before they react. A CD woman needs time to contemplate a disagreement, analyze the conversation, and figure out where things went wrong before she can move on to a resolution. This meditation is essential for a CD woman's counterpart to understand; the more they push a CD woman to express herself, the more she will clam up in response.

Fears Loss of Security

Finally, if your woman is a CD, she craves stability in her life, especially her finances. She will likely be frugal in her spending and make decisions with the lowest level of risk. At times, a CD woman may pick a job over family, not because she loves to work more, but because she needs security above all else. The hierarchy of basic needs for a CD woman is as follows:

- Career/Financial Security
- Hobbies/Children
- Relationships/Family
- Sex/Lovers

The position of each need doesn't equate to a lack of love and value for their partner/family. It means that it's essential for a CD woman to feel that she's providing security for herself, her family, and her partner before she can give her full attention to the next set of needs.

Deeper Dive into the Mountain Yeller (MY) Woman

If your woman is an extrovert, chances are she's been called that more than once in her lifetime. An extrovert is typically known for being outgoing and the life of any party. But there's so much more to them than meets the eye.

Outgoing Nature/Group Socialization

An MY woman is inherently outgoing. Her energy thrives on interactions and being around people as often as possible. Instead of needing time alone to recharge, an MY woman wants to be out and involved.

At a social event, MY women will be the first to initiate games and dancing and will often bounce from person to person, catching up rather than focusing on one task at a time. Deep conversations are still on the table but not at a social event. MY women are usually the ones who rally their friends for a group outing over a weekend rather than sitting at home reading a book or watching TV. Even in the workplace, MY women love group projects and find collaborative brainstorming and teamwork exciting.

Emotion-Driven

MY women are heart-ruled because they lead with their intuition and emotions. Being ruled by their heart doesn't mean their decisions are devoid of logic but rather that their feelings heavily influence their reactions. MY women can be emotional during arguments but are also the first to send a heartfelt message to a friend upon hearing they are having a rough time.

An MY woman's emotions will show throughout her storytelling, so be patient when she tells you about an event or relays the plot to a movie. Chances are both will be full of details and embellishments.

Connection and Touch

MY women crave genuine connections and physical touch. Whether a hug, a pat on the back, or simply holding hands. It reinforces their feeling of being connected. In a relationship, the MY woman will crave physical affection and see it as a top priority over other needs—something we'll discuss in depth a bit later.

Dynamic Focus

The MY woman is a natural multitasker. Instead of focusing on one task at a time, her attention shifts between assignments. She enjoys the energy she gets from juggling multiple projects and often gets bored working on one task for an extended period. It can be common to find the MY woman drifting off or needing to fidget during a long presentation.

The MY woman doesn't mind dealing with paperwork but will work through it while watching television or listening to music. As for conversations, the MY woman loves to chat, but don't be surprised if you find the MY woman scrolling on her phone while talking with you. It's not that the MY woman thinks what you have to say is unimportant. Her mind simply runs at higher speeds, and she's more comfortable when processing more than one thing at a time.

Inferential Communication

The MY woman often communicates using stories, anecdotes, and metaphors rather than getting straight to the point. She relies on indirect implications and expects others to infer meanings, which can confuse someone who may not be familiar with her communication style.

During an argument, the partner of an MY woman may find it hard to decipher what the MY woman really wants, even if she feels she has told them directly. It's essential to have a middle ground where communication is concerned, especially if your woman is an MY trying to get through to a CD. Their communication styles are very different.

Immediate Emotional Expression

Unlike their CD counterparts, MY women are quick to express their emotions. They're an open book and rarely hesitate to share their feelings of joy and disappointment. This expression can be overwhelming for a CD uncomfortable with an emotional display.

One of the greatest fears the MY woman faces is the fear of rejection. If an MY woman has a CD partner who pulls away at any sign of conflict, this can be a bone of contention. The MY woman will take your withdrawal as a sign of personal rejection. It's important to communicate that you are not rejecting her and that you simply need time to wrap your head around and process the disagreement. Give the MY woman verbal and physical affirmations whenever possible.

The hierarchy of basic needs for the MY woman is as follows:

- Relationships/Sex
- Family/Children
- Friends/Hobbies
- Career/Financial Security

If you are a CD and your partner is an MY, don't panic; it doesn't mean you can't have a successful relationship. There are plenty of affectionate and fulfilling relationships between opposites. It just means it will take time, work, and patience to learn one another's needs and effectively communicate.

The Straddler Woman

If your woman is a Straddler, she is adaptable and enjoys the best of both worlds. She can immerse herself in a book like a CD woman or be the life of a party like the MY woman. She possesses an emotional agility that allows her to straddle her personality types seamlessly. While this book predominantly focuses on CD and MY women, Straddlers can use it to understand the extremes and navigate their middle ground more effectively.

Excellent Balance Between Reflection and Expression

A Straddler woman can introspect like a CD, valuing quiet moments of thought. Yet, she also appreciates the expressive vitality of the MY and shares her feelings and ideas openly when a situation calls for it. She is as happy spending a quiet evening reading as she is going to a book club and actively participating in a lively discussion.

Adaptable in Social Situations

While she might not always be the life of the party, the Straddler woman easily adjusts to situations based on the social settings and the company involved. She can engage in a one-on-one conversation at a party and then join a group game or be the center of the party later in the evening.

Values Logic and Emotion

A Straddler woman approaches situations with a logical mindset but is equally attuned to emotional undercurrents, valuing the importance of feelings in decision-making. For example, if a colleague faces a personal issue, the Straddler woman will offer practical solutions while simultaneously providing emotional support.

Flexibility in Needs and Fears

The Straddler woman's hierarchy of needs will fluctuate based on circumstances, and she might experience fears from the CD's spectrum, such as loss of security, as well as the MY's fear of rejection. However, adaptability allows her to prioritize different aspects of her life. While working on an important business project, she will prioritize career stability, but in her downtime, she will focus on relationships and personal connections.

Fluid Communication Styles

A Straddler woman can communicate directly and inferentially, often adjusting her communication based on the recipient. For example, when conversing with her analytical boss, she will be direct and to the point, but when she talks to her best friend, she becomes expressive and delves into all the nitty-gritty details.

Straddlers possess an innate ability to mediate and find common ground, especially in relationships where CDs and MYs might find themselves at odds. Her adaptability enables her to comprehend and empathize with both personality types, easing communication and diminishing misunderstandings.

A Straddler woman and her partner may seem like a perfect match. However, everyone encounters their share of struggles. The flexibility of a Straddler often creates confusion about her preferences and needs. She might sometimes feel stretched or trapped in the middle, particularly in a polarized situation where she wishes to please her partner and struggles to voice her disagreements. A Straddler woman must discern what is significant to her while also learning to navigate her partner's personality type, much like everyone else.

So, How Do You Find Common Ground?

I'm a CD, and my partner is an MY. Is my relationship doomed?

Absolutely not! In this book, we don't tell you how to "cope" with your partner's differences. We provide you with the ability to realize the unique strengths each person brings to a relationship. A CD's introspection can balance an MY's spontaneity. An MY's vivacity and exuberance can harmonize beautifully with a CD's depth and stability.

Recognizing these different traits is merely the first step to a healthy relationship. The real challenge, and indeed the focus of this book, is to find ways to navigate the complexities of these interactions. After all, the beauty of a relationship is the elegant and empathetic dance between these personalities.

Key Takeaways

Diving into the intricacies of personality types isn't about affixing labels but rather enriching our understanding. With these insights, you're now armed with the necessary vocabulary to navigate the labyrinth of human emotions and connections, fostering an environment where love thrives, compassion blossoms, and relationships flourish. As we embark on this journey, let's remember that the goal isn't to change but to adapt, appreciate, and love more deeply.

The foundation for a nurturing relationship starts with understanding—understanding yourself, your partner, and the dynamics of your interaction. With the knowledge of CD and MY personality traits, you're well on your way to deepening that knowledge, setting the stage for the subsequent chapters that will guide you on how to cherish your partner in ways that resonate with both of you.

Understanding personality differences is essential for nurturing compatibility. This chapter has illuminated the fundamental traits of CDs, MYs, and Straddlers:

- **Reserved Nature:** Respect your CD partner's need for personal space and quiet reflection. Don't force immediate emotional reactions.

- **Logical Thinking:** Recognize your CD partner's analytical approach. Be patient as they process and express their feelings.

- **Singular Focus:** Acknowledge that multitasking is difficult for your CD partner. Allow them to complete or pause their task before they give you their full attention.

- **Emotion-Driven:** Empathize with your MY partner's emotions. Give your woman positive affirmations/compliments and physical affection.

- **Inferential Communication:** Listen for meanings implied indirectly in your MY partner's stories. Learn to read between the lines.

- **Dynamic Focus:** Accept your MY partner's wandering attention. Multitasking is their nature. If you need their complete focus, tell them.

- **Excellent Balance:** Appreciate the adaptability of a Straddler partner. Avoid putting them in the middle of conflicts.

- **Flexible Needs:** Accommodate shifts in a Straddler partner's priorities. Reassure them of your unconditional love.

The key is learning your dance as a couple. When personalities harmonize through compassion and respect, relationships flourish.

Chapter Two

Communication Is Key

A strong relationship takes more than just love. It requires a hearty helping of connection, understanding, and a whole lot of communication. After time sets in and the two of you have been together for a while, the "new relationship energy" quickly disappears. Your partner is no longer the magical woman who could do no wrong. She is now a human being with complex emotions and issues you may not have noticed when you first got together.

In this chapter, we'll dive into the depths of communication, showing you ways to make your bond stronger than ever. We'll also navigate the unique quirks of each personality type and how you can use indicators to validate your woman and her needs.

It's easy to be taken away by "the power of love." Still, the truth is that lasting relationships require a lot of effort, respect, and a willingness to comprehend things from another person's point of view that doesn't always align with your own. To do that, you must appreciate and respect your partner. This appreciation goes beyond just knowing her favorite snacks—it's about understanding her unique personality traits and how they work in tandem with your own.

With technology taking precedence over human interaction, it's important to remember the importance of patience, contemplation, and being there for our partners. So, as we move through this portion, take a break every now and then, reflect, and allow yourself to feel. By creating an atmosphere of trust and mutual admiration, you're not only forming a relationship, but constructing a friendship supported by empathy, kindness, and genuine communication.

Express Feelings Gently Without Starting Conflicts

Expressing your feelings is crucial for every relationship, but it's essential that we do so without triggering conflicts. It's all too easy to get wrapped up in our emotions when expressing them to someone else—especially when you're first sorting through them. So, first, take a step back, breathe, and formulate your thoughts before verbalizing them. You want to get your point across but you don't want your woman to feel attacked.

Remain Calm

Try not to overreact to difficult situations. By remaining calm, it's more likely that your woman will feel like she has the space and ability to consider your perspective.

Express Feelings with Words, Not Actions

If you start to get angry and feel you may lose control, take a break and do something to help yourself feel calm.

- Take a walk.

- Do breathing exercises.

- Interact with a pet.

- Journal.

- Read a book.

Address One Issue at a Time

Don't introduce tertiary issues until you've fully discussed the primary problem. This way, you'll avoid what experts call the "kitchen sink effect." Dr. John Mordechai Gottman (born April 26, 1942), an American psychologist and professor at the University of Washington, coined this term while working on divorce prediction and marital stability. The phrase describes the act of one partner throwing "everything but the kitchen sink" into an argument by dredging up past mistakes and grievances. This tactic is particularly counterproductive, as it's often overwhelming to the partner receiving the grievances.

Mitigate the Kitchen Sink Effect

When emotions flare up, it's natural to fall back on old hurt feelings—especially if they're similar to current difficulties.

- One of the most common reasons for someone to resort to "kitchen sinking" is quite simple: to win the argument. However, this amounts to "winning the battle but losing the war." It's a surefire way to sabotage potential progress in your relationship.

- Poor communication skills can also be to blame. Sometimes, a person doesn't realize they're being destructive by doing this, never having learned how to express and work through past feelings of hurt in a healthy manner.

Fixation of past mistakes is almost always counterproductive. Your woman may feel bullied, overwhelmed, or even blindsided by the onslaught of criticisms, especially if the argument is over something else entirely. If you resort to this tactic, it's indicative of avoidance. So, ask yourself: are you dodging the real issue at hand? Do you know what you're really upset about?

Instead of resorting to this method, remain calm and employ effective communication techniques. You don't want to bully your woman, no matter how angry you may be. Easier said than done, of course! It's a difficult habit to break, but if you find yourself participating in this behavior, the most important thing to do is remain aware and calm. If you value your relationship and want to move forward, choose your words mindfully and let go of past transgressions.

Resist Underhandedness

Avoid hitting below the belt or being underhanded. Never use these conversations to attack your partner—especially in sensitive areas. These attacks only foster distrust, anger, and harmful vulnerability. We don't want to "win" arguments. We want to work through issues by effectively communicating. Remember, it's not you versus her. It is you and her versus the problem.

Avoid Clamming Up

Positive results can only be obtained by way of proper communication. It can be easy to feel overstimulated and charged when discussing your feelings with your woman, especially if she has somehow upset you or you think she may be upset with you. Often, when emotions run high, we "clam up" or shut down as a defense mechanism.

It is important to note that when one of you becomes silent and stops responding, frustration and anger can soon take hold. If you feel yourself getting overwhelmed or shutting down, take a break from the discussion. Communicate with your partner that you aren't ready to continue the conversation, but reassure her that you will return to it as soon as you can. This honesty can help mitigate her anger by showing her you're feeling overwhelmed rather than allowing her to think that you don't care enough to respond.

The most important part of this process, though, is ensuring that you *do* return to the conversation. Follow-up is critical. Keep your promise and return to it as soon as you can recharge. You may even want to refer to the "remain calm" section to recenter for the next discussion.

Likewise, if you notice that *she* is clamming up, offer to circle back later to give your partner time to reset.

Be Specific and Productive

Be precise about what's bothering you. Try not to generalize. Avoid words like "never" or "always." These sweeping terms are usually inaccurate anyway and will (almost) always heighten tensions regardless of your woman's personality type. Instead of using hyperbolic language that could cause your partner to feel powerless, focus on what you're feeling in the moment. Vague complaints are also challenging to address, and productively tackling each specific item is essential.

Practice Active Listening

Practice active listening when she tells you something important, and avoid interrupting her when she's speaking, even if you might disagree. Active listening is the most important aspect of effective communication. It involves not just hearing her words but understanding her emotions and where she might be coming from. Validate her feelings and show you truly care about what she has to say by maintaining eye contact and providing non-verbal cues like nodding to show that you're engaged. Our body language matters; she'll know if you aren't engaged in what she's saying.

Be present in the conversation and take her feelings and criticisms seriously. Don't be distracted by external situations. Never multi-task while she is communicating with you. As much as she may appreciate the gesture, put down those dishes. Put away your phone. A good rule of thumb is to not engage in the activity if it takes your eyes or thoughts away from her.

Listen to and reflect on what she is saying before responding. Be sure to ask open-ended questions to encourage her to share more, and remember one thing: if she's communicating it with you, it's important.

Use Neutral Language to Avoid Escalation

We never want to make your partner feel attacked. Escalation will never end well, especially if something is bothering you. Emotions will flare, and you and her will say and do things you regret. When a situation is bothering you, make sure you make good communication choices. Your choice of words can significantly impact the tone of the entire conversation. To prevent defensiveness and promote understanding, avoid accusatory language and instead focus on the specific behavior or issue. Accusations will lead her to focus on defending herself rather than on understanding you and your perspective. Instead, discuss how an action made you *feel*.

Use "We" Statements

Using "we" instead of "you" statements conveys that you are in this together, working as a team to resolve the problem. Your partner needs to understand from the get-go that it is not you versus her. It is you and her versus the issue. It's important to communicate that you are practicing empathy and acknowledging each other's feelings and perspectives to maintain a harmonious relationship; using "we" language shows that it's your relationship against the problem and takes away the ideology that *she* is the problem.

For instance, if the issue is about you feeling overwhelmed or neglected intimately, using "we" statements can help you address the concern without making her feel accused.

Don't Say This:
"You never want to be intimate."

Instead, Say This:
"We seem to have a bit of a disconnect intimately lately. It's making me feel a little neglected. Can we find a way to meet in the middle or discuss where the disconnect may be?"

Emphasizing "we" makes the conversation more about finding solutions together rather than pointing fingers, which can often lead to a more productive and less confrontational discussion.

Use "I" Statements

Once again, avoid being accusatory. Expressing yourself without becoming overly aggressive can be challenging when faced with a conflict. To help de-escalate the situation and clarify your point, an "I" statement—or an assertive statement—is an effective psychiatrist-approved approach rather than making a blame-driven "you" statement.

Suppose there's a conflict where again you feel neglected, and let's say this time it has nothing to do with intimacy. Let's say your girlfriend or wife spends a lot of time working, and you feel like she isn't paying enough attention to you.

Don't Say This:
"You're always working and never spend any time with me! You don't care about our relationship."

Instead, Say This:
"I feel neglected when you spend a lot of time working, and we don't get to spend quality time together. I value our relationship and would like us to find a balance that allows us to enjoy each other's company."

This "I" statement expresses the speaker's feelings and needs without blaming or accusing your woman, thus making it more likely to result in a productive conversation rather than an argument.

Using language that emphasizes how *you* feel is much more effective communication and is less likely to result in her shutting down or getting angry. It also aids in her ability to empathize and see things from your perspective. Here's another example:

Don't Say This:
"*You never* want to go out anymore." (This is also likely a generalization.)

Instead, Say This:
"*I feel* frustrated that *we* don't seem to go out as often anymore. I would like it if *we* could work out a schedule that makes us both happy."

Speaking this way avoids tactics of attack, critique, and criticism, which usually lead to more hostility and defensiveness. In general, using "I" messages can create a constructive dialogue about the true causes of a conflict by avoiding aggressive behaviors and fostering effective communication.

Appreciate Silence and Peace with CDs

For the CD woman, silence is often a way to process her thoughts and emotions. It's essential to appreciate and understand this aspect of her communication style:

- Allow her the time she needs to gather her thoughts before discussing important matters.

- Avoid pressuring her to speak immediately after a conflict; she may need time to reflect first.

- Create a safe space where silence is not perceived as a negative response but as a part of the communication process. Encourage her to reflect for a while before discussing important matters.

Offer Verbal Affirmations and Reassurance to MYs

MY women thrive on verbal affirmations and emotional expression. Here's how to make your MY girlfriend or wife feel valued and loved:

- Compliment her genuinely and frequently. In fact, be her biggest fan! Even in front of family and friends.

- Tell her you love her at least once a day.

- Send an impromptu romantic text.

- Tell her how much you appreciate everything she does for you.

Understand and Be Mindful of Personal Boundaries

Both CDs and MYs have distinct personal boundaries. Respecting these boundaries is vital to a healthy relationship. Therefore, it's crucial to have open and honest discussions about your respective boundaries and comfort zones. You shouldn't push your partner beyond their comfort zone, whether they need personal space or social engagement—even if this level of care conflicts with your own needs. Creating a balance that respects both your and her needs for personal growth and reflection is a critical step in communicating and growing with each other. Establishing ground rules regarding when to compromise is a great idea when setting personal boundaries with one another.

Engage in Relationship and Emotional Check-ins

Regular relationship check-ins provide a platform to address concerns and strengthen your connection. These can be done as often as you need them to be done. Some couples do them every night, some once a week, and some may only check in once a month. Do what works best for your relationship! It may take a little time to find that perfect sweet spot, too, so don't be afraid to ask her if she feels you are checking in enough.

No matter how often, scheduling a dedicated time for these check-ins is essential to ensure they happen consistently (or at all). It's also imperative that these check-ins touch on the *positive* aspects of your relationship in addition to concerns. Specialists strongly recommend that each of you share something positive about the other during these sessions to help make these check-ins less like an argument and more about the two of you working together for a common goal. Remember, if you want to set aside time for her, then you indeed love her. Make sure you find positives about her and your relationship before engaging in a check-in. After you hype each other up and communicate your appreciation for one another, it's time to open the floor for all honesty. This will allow you to address areas of improvement and actively work together to adjust your relationship.

Make sure you are open to feedback and be ready to make changes and sacrifices for the sake of your relationship.

How Do You Do a Relationship Check-In?

Pick a Regular Time

Ideally, you'll both be relaxed, present, and in a good mood, so don't schedule a check-in after a long day at work or when you're short of time. You want to bring your best attitude and a clear mindset to these meetings with your partner.

Set the Scene

Your relationship check-in is an opportunity to slow down and connect, so why not make it feel a little special? To that end, bring your favorite snacks and drinks—and conduct the check-in somewhere that feels good to both of you. It must be a private and secluded atmosphere so you both feel comfortable getting real. Ordering take-out and planning something relaxing afterward can also help set the mood and feel like a great reward or incentive. However, do keep in mind that it is encouraged to have these conversations without the influence of alcohol.

Set a Time Limit

You don't want this to become a huge time sink, and you never want it to feel like a chore, so aim for a manageable timescale, especially in the beginning. These check-ins are about opening the lines of communication in a safe and calm manner; you might not resolve everything all at once. Rather, it allows you to create healthy

Celebrate and Appreciate Each Other

boundaries when expressing vulnerabilities in every facet of your relationship.

Always start with the positives of your relationship. This appreciation helps each partner remember why they're doing all of this in the first place! Giving compliments and joyful feedback upfront helps your partner feel comfortable and valued. This is especially necessary if there are more challenging topics to discuss afterward. Appreciation and validation are essential ingredients for a quality relationship.

Always Finish on a High Point

A celebration, even a small one, can be a fun way to wrap up the check-in. Remember, you aren't supposed to use these check-ins as a space to regurgitate everything your partner has done wrong since your last check-in. You should be having conversations about issues or wrongdoings as they happen. This is merely a time to check in on how everyone is doing and if there are still adjustments you both need to make. If you wait to vent during these check-ins, and these check-ins alone, you may be a powder keg next to an open flame—ready to explode!

Also, remember to end the session with a physical touch or an affirmation. Even if things get a little tense or something feels unresolved, find a way to return to each other and your overall belief in the relationship. If you're checking in regularly and discussing action items as they crop up, it's clear that your relationship is worth believing in.

Set Aside Time for Reflection and Understanding

Allocating time for personal reflection and understanding enhances self-awareness and empathy. It gives proper time for each person in the partnership to discover their unique needs in addition to their strengths and weaknesses. Admitting personal faults to ourselves—let alone others—isn't easy. So, consider setting aside moments for self-reflection. Specialists also recommend you journal these thoughts to understand your emotions better and to have the ability to look back at your progress. Encourage your partner to do the same, and share your insights with each other when you're ready.

Use this personal time to explore your progress and how those advancements align with your partner's journey of self-awareness. Self-awareness refers to a clear understanding of your own emotions, strengths, weaknesses, thoughts, and beliefs—and how they might influence your behavior, including your interactions with your partner. Self-awareness is fundamental for healthy relationships with yourself and others—especially romantic ones. Understanding ourselves means understanding our needs, expectations, boundaries, and communication styles. All of these shape how we interact and love our partners. When we're not self-aware, we open the door to harmful interactions due to blind spots in our communication and waning emotional health. A lack of self-awareness can lead to:

- Poor emotional regulation, which results in outbursts and other unhealthy expressions of anger or hurt.

- Personal neglect and impaired mental health.

- A skewed perception of reality due to biases and defense mechanisms that build up over time. (Also, without self-awareness, a person tends to reject constructive criticism, thus missing out on potential personal growth.)

- Communication blind spots.

- Crossing boundaries, whether your own boundaries or your woman's.

Being more self-aware gives us the tools necessary to have satisfying and successful relationships. It just makes sense. Know yourself, and you'll have the foundation for a life and relationship that isn't just surviving but thriving.

Embrace Spontaneity and Passion

Spontaneous gestures and surprises can add excitement to your relationship, particularly for MY women who appreciate such acts. Ways to embrace spontaneity include surprise outings or planning activities without revealing all the details in advance. Even if *you* know what will happen this time, perhaps your woman will reciprocate next time. Express your affection unexpectedly through notes, small gifts, and random acts of kindness. Your partner will appreciate the effort involved, and if they're especially fond of surprises, this could help them feel seen and validated.

Share Personal Growth Moments Regularly

You can begin to document your personal development using feedback from your scheduled meetings, emotional discussions, and self-awareness exercises. Once again, journaling is a great way to record feedback and your own reflections. It can provide a glimpse of previous versions of yourself and give greater insight into your personal growth.

Personal growth is an ongoing journey, and sharing these moments of realization—even epiphanies—with your partner can deepen your connection with your woman. Discuss your personal experiences, challenges, and lessons learned through self-reflection and check-ins with your partner. Nothing feels better than knowing we've helped someone, so when your woman helps, be sure to tell her!

Along the way, support each other's aspirations and encourage continued self-improvement exercises. Then, go on to celebrate milestones in your personal development journey together. By following these guidelines and strategies, you can improve your communication with your partner, whether she is a CD or an MY. Effective communication is the key to understanding, empathy, and building a strong and thriving relationship.

Key Takeaways

Effective communication forms the cornerstone of all healthy and flourishing relationships. It goes beyond the confines of personality types. This chapter has explored the fundamental facets of communication you can use to engage with your partner on a deeper level, whether they exhibit CD or MY characteristics.

Communication is the vital link that connects two souls—so never underestimate its importance.

- **Express, Don't Explode**: Voicing feelings is vital, but how you do it can make or break a conversation. Steer clear of the "kitchen sink" approach and tackle one concern at a time.

- **Listen and Hear**: True listening goes beyond catching words. It's about diving deep, reading between the lines, and feeling the heartbeat behind superficial language.

- **Narrate Neutrally**: Use "I" and "we" statements. These aren't just words; they're bridges that ensure your message gets across without raising defenses.

- **Pivot Your Personality**: Recognize the silence savored by CDs and shower MYs with affirmations that resonate.

- **Establish Clear Boundaries**: Establish them. Acknowledge them. Respect them. If they're different from yours, that's all right. Find the middle ground through open conversation.

- **Write Relationship Report Cards**: Periodic check-ins keep the ship steady. Use them as reflection mirrors, not boxing rings. And when solitude calls, answer—it fosters self-awareness.

- **Dance Freely**: Sometimes, unplanned moments make the most treasured memories. A little surprise can sprinkle in a whole lot of magic.

- **Share, Grow, Connect**: Sharing personal growth stories isn't just about telling tales—it's about weaving your growth narratives *together*.

Remember, it's not about speaking the loudest but resonating the deepest. Effective communication is the only way to proper understanding, empathy, and establishing a robust, healthy partnership. By applying these strategies, you can—and will—cultivate a more profound connection with your woman. As they say, it takes two to tango, and being conscious of your partner's steps is paramount!

Chapter Three

Enhance the Intimacy

When discussing intimacy in a romantic partnership, what usually comes to mind are physical acts. We think of kissing, holding hands, hugging, cuddling, and, of course—sex. While physical intimacy is integral in romantic partnerships, it isn't the only type of intimacy. Emotional intimacy and physical intimacy in a relationship are often linked, but one is no less important than the other.

Before we continue to examine and explore intimacy, it is important to recognize that each woman differs. While her personality type may influence some of these differences, there is no one-size-fits-all approach to any woman or relationship. Each person experiences and yearns for different types of emotional and physical intimacy.

If your relationship is just beginning, you may be just beginning to discover these preferences. Or perhaps you have journeyed well beyond the initial stages of your relationship, and you have come to understand that the puppy-love days are over. The woman you love and adore is no longer a picture of perfection. Instead, she is a complex human being with her own emotions and desires.

In this chapter, we will dive into the intimate aspects of your relationship and explore the fascinating dynamics that come into play when you're in love with a CD or an MY woman. These two personality types approach sex and intimacy differently, and by understanding their distinctive traits, you can unlock a deeper connection with your partner.

Understand Sexual Dynamics Between CDs and MYs

Understanding how sexual dynamics differ between CDs and MYs is an essential first step. These two personality types often approach sex and intimacy differently due to their distinct traits and needs. For instance, CDs tend to be more deliberate and focused on specific details. If your woman is a CD, she may prefer planned, structured intimacy. MYs, on the other hand, are often spontaneous, emotionally driven, and thrive on affectionate gestures. If your woman is an MY, she may express herself more naturally and passionately in situations where a CD woman may be a little more reserved. These differences are called intimate communication styles.

Learn the Different Communication Styles in the Bedroom

It is essential to know how communication styles play a significant role in sexual dynamics. For CDs, effective communication may involve clear discussions about her preferences, boundaries, and desires. CDs often value deeper conversations and one-on-one time. She is likely just as passionate about you as you are about her, but if you're an MY, she'll have a different sexual communication style. One you may not initially recognize.

Your CD woman has an independence about her that can be quite appealing. Still, it can come across as aloof and potentially less passionate if you don't understand her personality and how she expresses herself. Communication is key with her; she is an excellent listener and more attentive than her MY counterpart. This can lead to an incredible sexual connection, as she will truly listen to your needs and desires, allowing you to feel heard, understood, and completely satisfied. CD women are often incredibly thoughtful and reflective, which, if you learn to reciprocate (even if this isn't your personality type), leads to a deeper mutual understanding during intimacy.

In the case of MYs, their communication might be a little different. As stated before, an MY may come across as a little more passionate upfront. This is because her communication is generally just louder and more intense than a CD. MYs have no issue expressing their emotions or needs vocally and clearly. This vocalization can be incredibly exciting and energizing. MYs are often adventurous and can offer that same adventure in the bedroom. However, their tendency to be the center of attention can sometimes lead to neglecting your needs or prioritizing their own desires over yours. It's important to communicate and set boundaries to maintain a healthy balance with either personality type so you can both feel satisfied and safe in the bedroom.

Build an Emotional Bond with CDs

Emotional connection is vital for either personality type, but they can manifest differently in each. For the CD woman, emotional connection is the most important aspect of her relationship, and when she feels valued and connected, there is a deep, rewarding experience to be had.

Various ways to build a stronger emotional connection with your CD include:

- **Listening Actively**: Always give her your full attention, maintain eye contact, and use nonverbal cues to show you're engaged in the conversation. This validates her.

- **Acknowledging Her Accomplishments**: Celebrate her successes, whether big or small.

- **Providing Emotional Support**: Offer support by being patient, understanding, and empathetic.

- **Expressing Personal Goals**: Share your personal goals with her. This honesty will help her feel closer to you and will help her understand how your goals might align so that you can work together to achieve them.

- **Swapping Experiences**: Dive into new situations with her and experience things for the first time by her side. Even if it's something that makes you both a little nervous, overcoming that together can create a special bond.

- **Starting a New Tradition Together**: As you journey through your lives together, begin new traditions that are unique to your relationship.

- **Respecting Her Boundaries**: Whether your personality types are similar or not, make sure that you are always respecting the boundaries she communicates with you.

Highlight MYs' Need for Physical Closeness

Understanding and meeting the need for physical closeness in MYs is essential for fostering intimacy with them. MYs are naturally inclined toward physical affection, which means they often enjoy activities involving physical proximity or touch. This closeness is the way they communicate love, and it's also the way that they want to receive love. It is essential to meet your MY's needs in this way. Ways to validate her need for physical closeness include:

- Creating small, spontaneous acts of physical closeness.
    - Cuddle when you're watching a movie together.
    - Touch the small of her back while you're moving past her in the hallway or kitchen.
- Holding hands in public.
- Hugging her when she's upset or even when she's happy.
- Kissing her at any moment that makes sense, even in public.
- Being consistent.

Side note: while physical closeness is vital for MY's happiness, it's essential to have open and honest conversations about boundaries. Ensure that both of you are comfortable with the pace and boundaries you have set for physical affection and intimacy. Sometimes, a disconnect can occur when one partner is a CD and one is an MY, especially in the case of PDA (Public Displays of Affection). Let each other know if public hand-holding or hugging and kissing around others is appropriate, and discuss your comfort level for each.

Offer Surprise Romantic Gestures Catered to Each Type

Surprising your woman with thoughtful and romantic gestures is a fantastic way to nurture intimacy in your relationship. You can even cater these gestures to the unique personalities of both CDs and MYs.

Although MYs are often generally more open to surprises, CDs also appreciate romantic gestures and surprises from time to time. Understanding the preferences of your partner is critical. CDs and MYs often have distinct preferences when it comes to romantic gestures. MYs might appreciate grand gestures, while CDs may value more intimate, heartfelt acts. By understanding your partner's personality type and individuality, you can tailor your gestures to her preferences. You can create a deeper level of intimacy by being intimate in this way and ensuring that you are taking proper care to woo her with sweet gestures, whether big or small.

Surprise Gestures For MYs

Consider planning getaways, extravagant date nights, or big, bold, and elaborate romantic surprises. MYs often enjoy experiences that are visually stunning and memorable. Pull out the string quartets, the banners, the balloons, and the fireworks! The bigger, the better. Just ensure your love for her isn't lost in all the hoopla. Reaffirming your feelings for her and her place in your life during the gesture is key.

Surprise Gestures For CDs

Focus on small, thoughtful gestures. CDs often appreciate acts like cooking her favorite meal, having an intimate romantic picnic somewhere, leaving sweet notes around the house, putting together a fun scavenger hunt at home full of surprises, or arranging a cozy night on the couch. You can even arrange a massage to demonstrate your appreciation for her so she can relax beforehand. Most importantly, plan date nights that prioritize quality time together because that is what she will cherish the most.

Organize Thoughtful Date Nights

Creating memorable date nights is an excellent and entertaining way to enhance intimacy in your relationship. These special outings allow you to create memories together and spend much-needed quality time to foster the overall growth of your relationship.

Consider Individual Preferences

Make sure you consider your girlfriend's or wife's preferences before planning date nights. CDs may enjoy quieter, more intimate settings, while MYs prefer vibrant social engagements. If the two of you have different personality types, striking a balance between these preferences can lead to enjoyable experiences for both of you.

Alternate Date Responsibilities

When it's your turn to plan a date, make sure you fully take the reins on it, but if your woman is a CD and prefers to have a little more control, let her have some input if she wants it. To keep things interesting, take turns organizing surprise outings. These surprises add an element of excitement and ensure that you each get to experience the kind of date you enjoy, especially if you have different personality types.

Incorporate Variety

Keep your date nights interesting by incorporating variety into the mix. Fuse together your traditional dinner dates with more adventurous options. Instead of dinner and a movie, do dinner and a hike. Instead of a movie, go to a concert or a play. Try new hobbies together, stop repeating the same dates over and over again, and keep that spark alive!

Surprise Her

For MYs who appreciate spontaneity, adding surprise elements to your date nights can be a real treat. This could involve secret plans or unexpected stops during your outing. Head to a new bar for cocktails before dinner, or head to a new dessert shop instead of eating dessert at the restaurant. Another fun surprise element you can incorporate into your date with an MY is taking her somewhere to shop for an outfit before the date. However, don't let her choose what she's wearing when you get there! Switch it up and pick each other's outfits. This brings laughter, fun, and potentially a whole lot of trust into the relationship!

Choose Quality Over Quantity

It's not about how often you go on dates but the quality of the time you spend together. Ensure that during your date nights, you truly focus on each other. This means engaging in meaningful conversations and creating opportunities for emotional connection. Get off your phone and stop letting distractions take your time away from your partner. In today's digital age, it's easy to get distracted by phones and screens. Make an effort to unplug during your date nights. This will allow you to be fully present with your partner and deepen your bond.

Remember that the goal of these date nights is to strengthen your emotional connection, regardless of whether you're a CD or an MY. By planning thoughtful and enjoyable outings, you can create lasting memories and enhance your intimacy.

Take a Walk Down Memory Lane

Revisiting cherished memories and reliving special moments can be a powerful way to enhance intimacy. It is essential to highlight and remember significant milestones in your relationship. Celebrating important milestones in your relationship with meaningful surprises will make your girlfriend or wife feel validated, respected, and appreciated. You can commemorate wedding/relationship anniversaries or even small accomplishments with special gestures that honor your journey together. Here are some great ideas for your to consider:

- **Look at Photo Albums Together**: These albums can be from your relationship together or even your separate pasts before you met. Remember, our pasts tell a story of who we are. Sharing that with your partner creates an enriching bonding moment.

- **Create a Memory Jar**: This is a fun activity for couples of all ages, where each of you write down your favorite memories of the other on small sheets of paper and place them in a jar. (Pro Tip: Go through some of them during your check-ins to bring positivity to the meeting.)

- **Revisit Special Places**: These can be places special to each of you individually or to your relationship. Examples of this would include:

  - Favorite vacation spots.
  - Where you first met.
  - Location of your engagement or where you first became a couple.

- **Watch Home Movies**: Pull out old videos of your time together. These videos can be on a disc, a VHS, or even digital. It is recommended to broadcast it to a large screen, if possible, but regardless, make it an intimate experience. Create a comfortable sitting environment and set the mood with dim lighting.

While revisiting the past is important, focus on creating new memories together. Plan new dates that can become cherished memories for the future. If you find yourself without many photographs or videos of your relationship together, make new memories and snapshot them for later. The more time that passes in your relationship, the more beneficial these walks down memory lane are. This is because seeing special shared moments together reminds you of the love and connection that brought you together in the first place. It's a beautiful way for either CDs or MYs to nurture intimacy and strengthen their relationship.

Discuss Your Sex Life Openly and Honestly

An open and honest conversation about your sex life is crucial for maintaining a healthy and satisfying life inside the bedroom and out. This is true for both CDs and MYs. When you discuss this with your wife or girlfriend, you must approach this topic with transparency and sensitivity.

When individuals, whether they identify as CDs or MYs, choose to keep their concerns, desires, or frustrations about their sex life hidden, it can lead to a host of potential problems. First and foremost, it can create a disconnect between partners. Unresolved issues can simmer beneath the surface, causing emotional distance and resentment to build over time. This can harm not only the intimate aspects of the relationship but also the overall emotional bond.

Additionally, avoiding open communication can result in misunderstandings. Partners may misinterpret each other's needs or desires, leading to unmet expectations and dissatisfaction. This can create a cycle of disappointment that erodes trust and intimacy.

Conversely, when couples engage in open and honest discussions about their sex life, it can lead to wild benefits—sometimes quite literally! Sharing your thoughts, desires, and concerns with your partner can foster a deeper emotional connection. It allows both individuals to better understand each other's needs and preferences, leading to a more satisfying and fulfilling sex life.

Communication also provides an opportunity to address any issues or challenges that may arise. Whether it's addressing differences in sexual desire or exploring new aspects of intimacy, working together as a team can lead to creative solutions and increased satisfaction.

Moreover, open dialogue about sex can strengthen overall communication within the relationship. When couples feel comfortable discussing intimate matters, it often carries over into other aspects of their partnership, leading to improved understanding and harmony in all areas of their life together.

Create a Comfortable Environment

Find a private, relaxed setting where the two of you can talk openly without distractions or interruptions. It's essential to create an atmosphere of trust and safety and make sure it's in a closed and private area.

Choose the Right Time

Timing matters when discussing sensitive subjects like intimacy and sex, especially with your female partner. It doesn't matter if she is a CD or an MY. Timing always matters. Select a day when you both are free from stress and have ample time for the conversation. Avoid bringing up the topic in the middle of an argument or when one of you is preoccupied or busy with something else.

Surprise Your Partner with Special Gifts or Excursions

Surprising your partner with thoughtful gifts or excursions can add a much-needed spark to your relationship. Whether she is a CD or an

MY, these gifts and spontaneous adventures will show you how much you love spending time with her and how important she is to you.

Consider a CD's Preferences:

Respect Her Need for Solitude

CDs often cherish alone time. A considerate surprise could involve giving her the gift of solitude. Plan an evening where you take care of household responsibilities, and if you have children, make sure you arrange a babysitter or do an outing with them yourself, giving her some likely much-needed personal time.

Book a Relaxing Retreat

Research secluded cabins in nature where she can disconnect from the daily grind. Make sure there are amenities that you both enjoy there. A nice fireplace you can cuddle next to, a pool table you can shoot pool on while she reads out on the porch, or even a hot tub you both can relax in and enjoy quality time together. Surprising her with a weekend escape might be exactly what she needs to recharge.

Create a Personalized Reading Nook

If your CD woman enjoys reading, surprise her by setting up a personalized reading nook in your home. Choose a comfortable chair, add soft and warm lighting, and stock it with her favorite books or magazines (extra points if you add an area for some tasty snacks).

Organize a Stargazing Adventure

Grab a blanket and some snacks and enjoy the outdoors! Plan a stargazing night in a remote location away from city lights. Bring a telescope if you want a closer look, but the naked eye can also capture the moment. Don't forget her favorite snacks, and some drinks to make it a fun night away from the hustle and bustle of everyday life.

Consider an MY's Preferences:

Plan a Surprise Party with Friends

If your MY woman enjoys socializing, plan a surprise party with close friends and family. Coordinate with their loved ones to ensure everyone can attend, and keep it a secret until the big reveal. MYs love surprises!

Organize an Adventure Getaway

Surprise her with an adventurous weekend getaway. Choose destinations that offer thrilling experiences like hiking a rigorous trail, zip-lining, exploring a new city, and if she is particularly adventurous, add in a helicopter ride or bungee jumping experience. MYs often find excitement in new and dynamic environments.

Buy Her Something to Wear

MYs love attention. Buying her a special gift to wear—whether that be a beautiful dress she's been eyeing or stunning jewelry—a gift is sure to impress her. Complimenting her while she wears it will gain you even more points.

Realize There's More to Intimacy than Sex

Throughout this chapter, we have discussed various ways to become more intimate with your partner. Of course, a lot of this has extended past physicality. Still, it is important to reiterate that although sex is a significant factor in any relationship, intimacy is more than just sex.

Emotional, intellectual, spiritual, and non-sexual physical intimacy all play a large role in your relationship. There are several ways to explore these non-sexual intimate moments to aid in growing closer to your partner. These are some methods worth trying:

- **Emotional Intimacy**
    - Have open and honest communication.
    - Participate in active listening.
    - Share your dreams and aspirations.
    - Celebrate each other's achievements.

- **Mental and Intellectual Intimacy**
    - Discuss shared interests and current events.
    - Explore new topics together.
    - Read books or attend workshops together.
    - Take up new hobbies together.
    - Challenge each other in healthy debates (make it a game).

- **Spiritual and Soulful Connection**
    - Explore one another's values and beliefs.
    - Pray or meditate together.
    - Have philosophical discussions.
    - Be together when reflecting.
- Take a nature walk.
- Exercise together.

Discuss Desires and Needs Periodically

It is vital that the two of you discuss your desires and needs periodically. Start this discussion by sharing your own preference when it comes to intimacy. Be specific and clear about what you would like your sex life to look like. Make sure you tell her what you find pleasurable and what you'd like to explore or change. Use "I" statements to express yourself, focusing on your feelings so she doesn't feel attacked. Remember, sex is a very sensitive topic—but that doesn't mean it also can't be fun and exciting.

The best way to express your desires is to do regular check-ins with her (as covered in the previous chapter) and make sexual intimacy a point of discussion. This creates a great moment to explore one another and find new ways to connect. Share your interests and fantasies with each other since these can often evolve over time and be completely different than when you first met. Be open to adapting.

Encourage Her to Share

After you've expressed your thoughts and feelings, encourage her to do the same. Ensure that she feels safe and supported in sharing her desires, preferences, and concerns. As she speaks, ensure you are practicing active listening. This means giving her your full attention, maintaining eye contact, and showing empathy. Avoid interrupting or passing judgment. Ask open-ended questions to gain a deeper understanding of her perspective.

Address Concerns Respectfully

Address any concerns you have in the bedroom during this private conversation. If you feel like frequency is lacking, communicate that in a "we" statement to take the blame out of the equation. Likewise, if she raises concerns or challenges, respond with empathy and respect. Avoid becoming defensive or dismissive. Instead, acknowledge her feelings and work together to find solutions or compromises that enhance your sexual connection.

Respect Boundaries

While communicating with your partner, it is essential to recognize that boundaries are important. If she is uncomfortable discussing certain aspects of intimacy with you, then you need to respect her boundaries and give her space. You can revisit the topic when she is ready.

Celebrate Intimacy

Lastly, celebrate the fact that you are intimate in a way that merits this discussion! Celebrate your relationship! Express gratitude to her and affection for her and her willingness to always work on this with you. This expression is a bonding exercise that can grow your relationship tenfold if done properly, making the intimate moments together that much more powerful.

Remember that discussing your sex life openly and honestly is an ongoing process. It's an opportunity to deepen your connection and enhance mutual satisfaction. While it might initially feel awkward to discuss this subject openly, over time, your ability to communicate with your partner on all sorts of topics will build a strong foundation of trust that will carry you through both trying and fun times and enhance the love and affection you have for one another.

Key Takeaways

As we explored the intricacies of intimacy, we also focused on the unique dynamics between CDs and MYs. Recognizing the sexual dynamics specific to both personality types and beyond is the first step toward building a fulfilling, intimate life with your woman. Personality types have distinct preferences and needs, which should be acknowledged and addressed, but it's also important to recognize your girlfriend or wife as the individual she is and cater to her needs specifically.

Every relationship requires intimacy, as it is the foundation of every relationship and is the key difference between your partnership and any other relationship that you have in your life. It is essential to:

- **Consider your partner's Preferences**: Highlight an MY's need for physical closeness and a CD's desire for communication.

- **Offer Tailored Romantic Gestures**: Your partner's ideal romantic gesture will vary depending on her personality type and personal preference. To really woo her, step out of the box and think about her likes and desires. Remember that a gesture doesn't have to be big if it's meaningful.

- **Organize Date Nights**: Don't let yourself or your relationship get stuck in a cycle. Think of new and exciting activities to do together. Even small changes can make a big impact.

- **Take a Walk Down Memory Lane**: Pull out those photo albums and home videos. Enjoy your past history, individual and shared. This can help you both come up with new things you would like to do together or experiences you want to repeat.

- **Discuss Your Sex Life Openly**: Sex is an intimate act, but don't let talking about it become taboo. Share your boundaries, likes, dislikes, and hopes. Having this discussion outside the bedroom can make what you do inside intimate, fun, and safe.

- **Appreciate and Surprise Your Partner**: Let your partner know how much they mean to you. Tell them with words, write them a note, or give them a gift.

- **Create Intimacy Outside of Sex**: Realize that there is more to intimacy than just sex. Share intimacy in other areas of your life together—whether this is physical, intellectual, or spiritual. Find ways to connect with one another throughout your day to express your love and affection for one another.

- **Respect and Celebrate Boundaries**: Ensure you discuss your desires and needs periodically. Celebrate this discussion. Respecting each other's boundaries builds a solid foundation of trust and compassion that will strengthen your relationship and affection.

Intimacy involves emotional and physical aspects; understanding her personality type helps cater to her needs effectively, but doing your regular check-ins, participating in active listening, and truly hearing her will give you a better and more specific scope on how to be intimate with her. By applying these insights and strategies, you can enhance the intimacy you have with your partner, no matter what your personality types are.

Chapter Four

Balancing Social Lives

In this chapter, we will embark on an exciting journey that many people in a relationship often forget to focus on: the importance of balancing your and your partner's social lives and how understanding the personalities of CDs and MYs aids in this attempt. This chapter focuses on how the two personality types thrive under different levels of social involvement and how it may affect your relationship.

Complement CDs' Need for Solitude with MYs' Social Inclinations

Understanding and accommodating the distinct social needs of CDs and MYs is crucial to the overall mental well-being of you and your partner, inside your relationship and outside of it. While CDs tend to seek solitude and personal space for introspection and recharging, MYs often thrive in social settings, delighting in vibrant interactions.

The foundation of any successful relationship is open and honest communication. Initiate a conversation with your partner about your respective social needs. CDs should express their need for occasional solitude and MYs their desire for social engagements. Sharing these feelings fosters understanding and allows for compromises to happen.

Negotiate Personal Space

CDs require alone time to rejuvenate. Encourage your CD partner to communicate when they need solitude and respect their space during these moments. MYs can use this time for their personal social interactions, allowing both partners to meet their needs.

Create a Relaxing Home Environment

Designate a tranquil space within your home where CDs can retreat when they need solitude. Make it comfortable and conducive to relaxation, ensuring it serves as a recharging space or sanctuary for them.

Balance Your Social Calendar

If you're an MY and she's a CD, balance your social activities between her solitude time and your socializing. Consider having specific days or times for social engagements together and then times for her to have her personal reflection. This way, both of you can feel validated and have your social needs met.

Support Each Other's Choices

No matter where you or her fall in your personalities, support one another even if you aren't thrilled with the choice your partner has made. For example, if she is a CD and expresses a desire for solitude while you want to go out, it's recommended that you respect her wishes and don't try to push her to join your social outing. Remember, if she's communicating her needs, they're likely important to her. You can ask her to engage in a social event with you at another time. Planning social outings in advance can help ensure that your CD partner is mentally and emotionally prepared for the event.

Set Realistic Expectations

Recognize that striking a balance between going out and staying in (if you differ in personality types) might require compromise. CDs may need to step out of their comfort zone occasionally, while MYs may need to accept that solitude is essential for their partner's well-being. Each partner will need to be flexible for the relationship to flourish.

Plan Activities Catered to Each Personality

In a relationship, planning activities that cater to both partners' personalities can be a great way to ensure each person's needs are met while simultaneously strengthening your bond. CDs and MYs have distinct preferences, and finding a middle ground can be difficult if your partner has an opposite personality. Still, when you find that common ground, your connection to her can become seriously enhanced.

Discuss Interests

It is important to initiate conversations about your hobbies and interests together. At the same time, remember that CDs often enjoy solitary or small-group activities like reading, hiking, and crafting, while MYs might be inclined toward social outings like dining with friends, attending parties, or participating in group sports. Understanding each other's interests is the first step in planning activities you can participate in together.

Compile a Shared List

Create a list of activities that interest both of you. These could include weekend hikes in nature, cooking classes, movie nights, volunteering, or even trying a new hobby together. Focus on activities that you both enjoy first – some common ground – and then make plans to do those things!

Schedule Regular "Me Time"

Acknowledging that both of you may need your own personal "me time" is essential to making a relationship work for the long haul. CDs may need occasional alone time for introspection, and MYs may crave social interaction that their partner may not want to engage in at the moment. Plan your schedules to include designated "me time" so that each of you can pursue your individual interests. This "me time" is a great time to take part in activities your partner just doesn't want to engage in.

Rotate Activity Choices

Alternate between activities that align with CDs' and MYs' preferences. For instance, if you enjoyed a social event one weekend, plan a quieter, more reflective activity for the next date. It's all about compromise and communication. If both your weeks have been stressful, engage in a safe activity you both know you'll enjoy. On the other hand, if you've both had plenty of time to rest, try pushing each other to try something fun and exciting.

Experiment with New Experiences

Keep the relationship with your woman fresh and exciting by occasionally stepping out of your comfort zone and encouraging her to do the same. Trying new things together can be an adventure that strengthens your bond. Whether it's taking a dance class, exploring a new hiking trail, or attending an art exhibit, she'll definitely appreciate your efforts in keeping everything interesting.

Balance Frequency

Ensure a balance between activities that cater to each personality. Avoid overwhelming your CD partner with frequent social events or leaving your MY partner feeling isolated. Open communication is key to finding balance. Make sure you follow previous recommendations on how to open a dialogue if either of you feels like there is an imbalance and wants to address a concern.

Reflect and Adjust As Needed

Periodically review how both of you feel and communicate any concerns. Have your own thoughts about the balance of your activities and whether you feel represented in your dates, and ask her to do the same. Be willing to adjust your approach based on her feedback. After all, participating in activities that you both enjoy—even if you differ in personality types—can foster an understanding between the two of you and strengthen your relationship. At the end of the day, we all want to feel heard and understood by the person we love.

By valuing each other's personalities and trying to accommodate each other's preferences, you'll strengthen your connection and create lasting memories together.

Life is all about adventures. Trying new things and embracing the fact that you are both unique individuals with your own interests will make your lives together happier and healthier. It can even make it that much more exciting and adventurous. Just make sure you celebrate her passions and encourage her in all of your endeavors together.

Gradually Introduce CDs to Social Settings

CD women often prefer solitude and may feel uncomfortable or overwhelmed in social settings. If your partner is a CD, introducing her to such environments and remaining by her side the entire time can be a thoughtful and considerate way to support her. Reassure her and stay near her the entire time, especially if you're the type to really enjoy social experiences and want to introduce her to your world or if you're the only person she'll know there.

Start Small

Begin with low-pressure social situations. Invite a few close friends or family members over for a small gathering at your home, informing your CD partner in advance so they can mentally prepare. Sometimes, as an MY, you will want your CD partner to engage in social activities with you. Consider opting for a "quality over quantity" situation when this happens. Smaller gatherings may be less intimidating and even enjoyable to her.

Communicate

Have an open conversation with your CD wife or girlfriend about her discomfort in social settings before you put her into one. Understand all her concerns and fears. Be patient and empathetic, and assure her that you'll be there to support and guide her through the entire process.

During this discussion, it's also important that you set expectations with her. Let her know exactly what she can expect on these outings. Share information about the schedule, who will be present, and what activities will be planned. Maybe even come up with a code word she can tell you if she's feeling uncomfortable and wants to leave early. Providing a clear picture can help alleviate her anxiety.

Offer Support and Take Breaks

Be a source of comfort for your CD woman during social events. Put yourself in her shoes and empathize with how she might be feeling. Make sure you stay close to her throughout the evening, introducing her to others and engaging in conversations when she's ready. It doesn't have to feel like a chore or that you're babysitting her, but do be conscious that she's outside her comfort zone and will likely want you there as a buffer to reduce stress.

Most importantly, remember that her need for solitude isn't a rejection of you but a reflection of her personality. Recognize that she might need a break from social interactions because they can be draining for her. Allow her to step away as often as she needs to recharge. If needed, devise a signal that lets you know when she needs some time alone.

Celebrate Small Wins

Acknowledge and celebrate her when she makes an effort to go to a party or a social interaction that she's nervous about. Express your pride and appreciation! This will encourage her to attempt future events.

Plan Post-Event Debriefs

After attending the activity, have a post-event debriefing session with her. Ask her how she felt and if she had fun. Discuss what she felt went well and what she might have found challenging. Use that feedback to plan for future events. It's entirely possible your CD woman enjoyed herself and doesn't need coaching or further aid. Just because she's a CD doesn't mean she doesn't like to talk to people. It just means she might just need a longer reset before the next event. On the flip side, it could be entirely possible that it was overwhelming. Make sure you ask her opinions and go from there.

However, gradually introducing her to these sorts of social engagements will help her get used to them. Remember to be patient regardless of the feedback you receive. Show her your support and celebrate her progress and her compromise by going with you in the first place. It took her a lot of energy and possibly even discomfort to go outside her comfort zone. If you're patient, you can ease her into social situations and create a perfect balance between her needs and yours.

Appreciate MYs' Need for Exciting Social Engagements

MYs thrive on social interactions and exciting experiences. If your woman is an MY, it's crucial that you understand and respect her need for lively social engagements, even if it isn't your thing. MYs' enthusiasm is infectious, so hopefully, that won't be an issue, but it's important to help her feel affirmed in the relationship. Make sure you embrace her zest for life and be open to trying new things. Your willingness to participate in her adventures can only strengthen the bond you have with her.

Recognize Her Energy and Support Her Social Initiatives

MYs often bring a lot of energy to social situations. Even if it isn't your thing, acknowledge and celebrate the qualities she brings to the table. Understand that her being enthusiastic about socializing is part of who she is. Encourage her to pursue social activities she might be passionate about. This could be joining clubs, attending parties or events, or going out with friends. No matter what it is, make sure that you're supportive.

Make sure you accompany her to social gatherings, even if they're outside your comfort zone. Your presence can provide her with a sense of security and make social events more enjoyable for both of you.

MYs enjoy excitement and new experiences. If you want to support her and show your affection, make her happy by planning outings or adventures that align with her interests. These outings could be hiking an adventurous trail with you and a group of her closest friends, dancing at the club, or exploring new places. Whatever it is, share in her enthusiasm for fun and adventure.

Remember, MYs appreciate spontaneity, so surprise her with unplanned outings or unexpected plans. These surprises can inject excitement into your relationship, make her feel valued, and affirm that the spark is still alive.

Create a Social Calendar

Work with her to create a social calendar that includes events and outings catering to both your personalities. This calendar will ensure that both partners have opportunities to engage in activities they enjoy. If hers is social and yours is more relaxed, you can plan that out beforehand so everyone feels they're being accommodated.

Set Healthy Boundaries

Just like in any other aspect of your relationship, as you balance your social lives, set healthy boundaries that you both respect.

While supporting your MY partner's social inclinations, setting personal boundaries is crucial to prevent burnout. This is especially true if you're a CD and she's an MY. Communicate when you need alone time or when certain social events may overwhelm you. Maintaining healthy boundaries is essential for everyone. To set them, it's important to:

- Have open discussion.

- Define what your personal space is.

- Maintain mutual respect for your partner and their wishes.

- Set clear expectations.

- Negotiate compromises.

- Respect non-negotiables (items that you absolutely cannot compromise on due to the level of discomfort it causes one of you).

Engage in Joint Activities, Both In and Outside the Home

When you're in a relationship, especially for a long time, it can be easy to fall into repetitive patterns. Generally speaking, many couples find themselves in a rut and may become couch potatoes in their relationship. While inside activities are relaxing, it is vital that you engage in activities outside of the home as well. Going outside is not only health for your relationship but for your own individual mental health as well, even if you're a CD who prefers to be at home.

Finding the proper balance between solitude and social engagements may be difficult in a relationship with one CD and one MY, but it is crucial. This could very well be one of the biggest obstacles in many "opposites attract" style relationships. Engaging in activities together, both at home and outside the home, can help bridge the gap between these personality types, so compromises generally need to be made.

Likewise, suppose two CDs are in a relationship together. In that case, it can become abundantly easy for the two of them to fall into a routine of staying home every night and never seeing the outside world together. Remember, spending time together is essential, and it might be easy to fall into a routine, but make sure you mix up your nights from quiet evenings to more social gatherings, no matter where you and your partner fall in your personality types.

Explore Shared Interests

Make sure you sit down together and explore hobbies and interests that both of you enjoy. This could be anything from cooking and gardening to playing video games. Make a list of your likes and plan to incorporate them into regular date nights.

Plan Regular Date Nights

Don't just make a list and put it to the side. Schedule regular date nights and be consistent with them. You both need time to connect and have fun together as a couple. These date nights don't always need to involve extravagant outings; they can be as simple as cooking a meal together, watching a movie, or stargazing. Choose things you both enjoy doing, alternating as often as possible.

Balance Quiet and Social Outings

Strive for a balance between quiet, introverted activities and more social experiences. For example, you can plan a cozy evening at home followed by an occasional dinner party with friends. You can even shake it up a bit and try:

- Attending workshops or classes.
- Volunteering.
- Joining clubs together.
- Taking a day trip to a nearby town

Share Responsibilities and Rotate Them

To ensure that both partners have a say in planning activities, take turns on who plans date night and discuss alternating nights between staying in and going out. This way, both of you have your preferences considered. This rotation is especially helpful if you and your woman have different personality types. That extra input can help create a balance in the relationship. It also alleviates burnout by preventing one partner from consistently being the one to choose and plan dates.

Create a Home Sanctuary

For your nights in, try to make your home as comfortable and inviting as possible. If you have a CD woman, create areas for relaxation and solitude and have a separate space to come together for quality time. Helping out around the house by completing chores before the date can help make your CD woman feel even more appreciated and allow these dates to become even more relaxing and intimate.

Allow Nights Out with Friends and Loved Ones

Navigating the social aspects of a relationship between CDs and MYs involves recognizing and respecting each other's need for time with friends and loved ones outside of your partnership. Start by having an open and honest conversation about your social needs and expectations. CDs may prefer solitude, while MYs thrive in social interactions and crave time with their friends or family. Discuss how you can strike a balance that works for both of you.

Support Individual Friendships

Encourage and support each other's individual friendships. Understand that it's healthy for both of you to maintain connections with your own circle of friends. You don't have to spend every free moment together. In fact, it's healthy to keep your individuality in your relationship.

Schedule "Friend Time"

If you feel like you need to set aside specific days or evenings for individual friend time, then communicate that with her. Agree on a regular schedule that allows each of you to spend time with your friends without causing friction in the relationship. Some women may have a girl's night tradition, and you may even have specific times you traditionally hang with your friends. Both of you should be able to participate in those without guilt.

Respect Personal Space

Respecting personal space is important for all personality types. While CDs may appreciate more personal space than MYs, both personality types can enjoy their space from time to time. One thing that the two of you can do to ensure you're both getting enough personal space is plan one partner's friend night during a time that the other can stay home and enjoy some quiet.

If you have a CD woman and you're an MY, a great suggestion might be to buy her a new book, draw her a bubble bath, and allow her time to soak while you go out for a drink with your friends. This solution respects the need for solitude in CDs and the social inclinations of MYs.

Engage in Mutual Social Events

When you're in a relationship, it can be difficult to juggle time with your friends, your family, and the two of you. You may feel overwhelmed and like you're spread too thin. A great way to alleviate this feeling is to make plans that include your and your partner's friends. A group outing this big can be difficult if they are entirely too different, but generally, you may find it a great way to integrate social circles and create a greater sense of togetherness.

Set Boundaries and Trust Her

Establish boundaries and guidelines for nights out with friends. Discuss topics like curfew, communication you may not be comfortable with her engaging in, and any expectations for afterward. Setting boundaries is best done in an open-forum conversation between both of you and not a list of demands.

Expressing your feelings and boundaries positively and appropriately will reduce any misunderstandings or arguments the two of you might have. After you express your boundaries, ensure you show her you trust her.

Trust is essential in any relationship. Trust that she genuinely values your relationship and that she wouldn't jeopardize it. Recognize that independence and time apart can strengthen your bond when you come back together.

Avoid Guilt Trips

It's important not to guilt-trip her for spending time with friends or for needing personal space. Respect her autonomy and remember that you both benefit from a well-rounded social life and occasional time away from each other.

Celebrate Reunions

Just as you would celebrate a special occasion, celebrate the time that you and your wife or girlfriend come back together. Plan a special activity or simply spend quality time together to reconnect and reinforce your bond.

Allowing nights out with friends and loved ones is a healthy way to balance the social needs of both CDs and MYs. It promotes trust, independence, and personal growth while also strengthening the relationship by valuing your individuality and social connections.

When you reunite after spending time with friends, share your experiences and stories. It'll give you something new to discuss by talking about your night. This sharing keeps the lines of communication open and helps both of you feel connected even though you weren't physically present during their outing.

Host or Attend Social Events or Gatherings

A great way to balance your social life involves participating in or hosting social events and gatherings.

Host Social Events

Collaborate with her to plan parties. This collaboration is a bonding exercise but also allows you both to have a say in the type of event, the guest list, and the overall experience. Integrate elements that cater to you both. Make your party a perfect combination of the two of you. Show off your relationship and focus on each of your strengths.

Attend Social Events

Attending social events or parties together can be fun. If she's the type to be fueled by interactions with others or dressing up, make sure you accommodate that by attending these parties as often as you can with her. If there is a disconnect in comfortability in social situations, make sure that you discuss your preferences and boundaries beforehand. Agree on a signal or a plan for when one partner needs to leave or take a break.

Create Traditions

Whether you're hosting or attending an event, consider making something a tradition that the two of you share. If you're hosting with her, plan to make the event an annual one. You could also create a special dish you recreate for all your events or even a special cocktail. Another suggestion might be to wear a signature outfit or to have a tradition of always matching or dressing in a way that complements one another.

Celebrate Milestones Together

Celebrating milestones together is essential to nurturing a healthy relationship. Begin by acknowledging the milestones in your relationship, both big and small. This could include anniversaries, personal achievements, or any date that may be important to either of you. Decide together how you want to celebrate each milestone to ensure you're both on the same page. Some CDs may prefer quieter celebrations, while MYs might enjoy larger gatherings or elaborate surprises. Talking about this beforehand can defuse any potential issues later.

Add a Personal Touch

Infuse each celebration with a personal touch that reflects both of your personalities. For example, if it's an anniversary, consider combining elements of each of you. Spend quality time together and enjoy one another and all the great things each of you brings to the table.

Create Traditions

Like social engagements, creating traditions together is therapeutic for the relationship. Consider traditions for celebrating significant milestones and be consistent. Recreating certain aspects of your first date can be a fun and exciting way to celebrate your anniversary. For example, on your anniversary, consider going to the restaurant you might have gone to on your first date. Traditions create a special bond between the two of you and can help keep that spark burning.

Capture Memories

Document your milestones and celebrations with photographs or keepsake items. These tangible reminders can help you both cherish each other for years to come, and they're great ways to share your special moments with family and friends who love you and are invested in your relationship.

Initiate Future Plans

When you celebrate milestones, take the opportunity to discuss them together with your partner. Reflect back on your past together and talk about where your relationship is going. If you're married, talk about your shared goals and dreams and how you can use these to grow closer as a couple. Think about what you want the coming year or years to look like and what new adventures you want to embark on together.

Extend Celebrations

Consider extending the celebration of your milestones beyond a single day. You can celebrate for a weekend or even a week. Make it a getaway and allow one another to fully immerse in your enjoyment of each other.

Acknowledge and Praise Individual Achievements

Acknowledging and praising individual achievements is an essential aspect of showing her that you respect her. Our social bonding is formed through several interactions throughout our lives. Most of it is formed by how people we care for respond to us in moments of pain and joy. If someone comforts you when you hurt, you begin to trust them. When someone celebrates you and jumps for joy as if your win was their win, you recognize them for caring about your successes.

Unfortunately, when one partner is doing well, the other partner might feel a reduction in their self-esteem, leaving them with a negative emotion to work through. It's crucial that you not let this type of emotion prevent you from loving or celebrating your wife or girlfriend when anxiety or envy rears its ugly head. Do your best to avoid jealousy so you can operate as her partner and best friend. Do this by creating an environment where both of you feel safe to pursue your goals, share your achievements, and avoid competing. Instead, focus on mutual support. Discuss your long-term visions and how you can support each other's growth and aspirations over time. This includes considering how your individual goals align with your shared goals as a couple.

Acknowledge Your Feelings

Maybe you are over the moon about your partner's achievements! If so, then that's wonderful! Maybe, though, you feel a few negative emotions from it. You might even feel a little guilty about having those mixed emotions. However, accepting your reactions and emotions for what they are will help you to make constructive changes. Honestly, these feelings usually have nothing to do with your partner at all but rather your own insecurities. Make sure you're honest with yourself about what you are feeling and why so that you can learn to grow as a person and become someone who can fully support your partner.

Resist Making Comparisons

You may be causing your own distress by ruminating over how you compare to your significant other—or, even worse, other people. When our partner does what we deem "better" than ourselves, we wonder if they may be looking elsewhere for a mate. Instead of comparing yourself to others, devote yourself to developing your own potential.

Respect and Enjoy Your Differences

You and your partner probably excel in separate areas. That is wonderful and the reason that partnerships can ultimately be so powerful. Understand your partner's individual goals and aspirations and draw on her strengths. Let her achievements and success give you the energy to chase down your own aspirations.

Support Her Accomplishments

It is important to always support your partner for who they are and the accomplishments they achieve. The best way to do this is by offering praise. The same compliments someone else gives her will mean so much more coming from you. You are the person she loves. Speak positively to her and offer genuine praise and encouragement. Express how proud you are of her accomplishments and the growth you've witnessed as she worked toward achieving this goal. Don't limit celebrations to major achievements either; acknowledge and celebrate small victories as well.

We want to congratulate her on getting an "A" on the test rather than only congratulating her when she graduates. Recognizing everyday accomplishments can create a positive atmosphere of encouragement, leading to bigger and grander achievements. Think of it as fuel. The more gas you pump into your tank, the further your car will go. Supporting her every step of the way will give her extra confidence and the drive to keep going.

Recognize her efforts even if there have been setbacks and learning experiences along the way. Be proud of her for trying. Remind her that you're on her side, even when she's struggling. A great way to be supportive during this is to offer to pitch in or lend a hand where you can. If she has a tight deadline or heavy workload, take on some extra household chores to alleviate stress and give her a lighter plate.

Giving your time to help her is being generous in a way that will show her your love. The more you build her up, the happier she will be, and the more she will trust you as her partner and support system. When you see she has succeeded, take the time to celebrate her. Tell her that you recognize the effort, dedication, and perseverance she went through to reach that goal, tailoring how you celebrate her preferences.

Key Takeaways

In this chapter, we dove into the intricacies of balancing social lives within the context of relationships while focusing on the dynamics of both CDs and MYs. Every individual has their unique social inclinations, and understanding and respecting these differences can lead to a fulfilling partnership.

- **Complement CDs' Need for Solitude with MYs' Social Inclinations**: Acknowledge that CDs often require solitude and personal space to recharge, while MYs tend to thrive in social settings. Finding a balance that respects both needs is key.

- **Plan Activities Catered to Each Personality**: Tailoring your social activities to the preferences of both CDs and MYs, as well as the two of you individually, ensures that both of you can enjoy your time together.

- **Gradually Introduce CDs to Social Settings**: For CDs who may be less inclined to attend social gatherings, gradual exposure and gentle encouragement can help them feel more comfortable in these outings.

- **Appreciate MYs' Need for Exciting Social Engagements**: MYs often enjoy exciting and dynamic social events. Recognize and participate in activities that cater to their preference to keep MYs energized and happy.

- **Set Healthy Boundaries**: Establishing clear boundaries for personal space and social interactions is essential. If both of you aren't social butterflies, these boundaries will help keep you comfortable. Just be sure you are both being honest about your comfort zones.

- **Engage in Joint Activities, Both in and Outside the Home**: Explore shared hobbies and interests, both within the home and in outdoor settings. Mix it up and enjoy each other no matter your personality types. Be sure to take turns planning dates to alleviate burnout.

- **Allow Nights Out with Friends and Loved Ones**: Recognize the importance of individual time with friends and family as well as maintaining a sense of individualism. Allowing each other to have occasional nights out can strengthen your relationship. Just make sure you celebrate coming back together.

- **Host or Attend Social Events or Gatherings**: Participate in social events as a couple or host gatherings, providing opportunities to strengthen your bond and share experiences with others. Show off your unique qualities and what makes you a great couple by collaborating with one another to plan parties.

- **Celebrate Milestones Together**: Celebrate personal or shared milestones, as it is a great way to acknowledge your past and plan for your future.

- **Acknowledge and Praise Individual Achievements**: Recognize and support each other's individual achievements. Celebrating her successes strengthens her trust in you and the love you share with each other.

Chapter Five

Resonating Emotionally

In this chapter, the treasures of emotional strength each partner brings to the table and the art of celebrating these strengths are brought to light. Understanding the emotional nuances of your woman is abundantly important whether she is a CD or an MY. We will dissect the differences each of these personality types portrays and how to meet them in a way that ensures both of you feel fulfilled and supported. We will teach you how embracing the differences each of you brings to the table makes for a strong and successful relationship. And together, we will navigate through strategies to identify, acknowledge, and complement these emotional strengths.

Celebrate the Emotional Strengths Each Type Brings to the Partnership

Celebrating the emotional strengths each partner brings to the relationship is essential for bonding and growth. To love your woman more effectively, resonate with her emotionally.

Identify Emotional Strengths and Compliment Them

Take the time to identify and acknowledge the unique emotional strengths each of you has. CDs often bring introspection, empathy, and stability, while MYs may contribute enthusiasm, spontaneity, and optimism. Recognize how your emotional strengths complement hers and vice versa.

CDs can provide a stabilizing presence during challenging times, while MYs can infuse energy and positivity into the relationship where negativity could quickly take over. are part of people's identity, and we often look for these traits during the dating process. Learn to appreciate these differences because oftentimes, these differences coincide with different emotional strengths as well.

Two partners having different emotional strengths is quite a good thing because it can allow the relationship to become more stable over time. This stability is due to the fact that each partner can feed off of the other's energy. Where one partner lacks, the other can cover the bill, and vice versa. Even if you share a personality type, you and your partner can still bring different strengths to the relationship. Personal interest, knowledge, and communication can all add to the emotional health of the relationship.

Express Gratitude

Regularly express your gratitude for her and her emotional strengths. If you've had a particularly bad day and your MY girlfriend or wife has supported you by adding an upbeat and optimistic breath of fresh air into your lungs, make sure you acknowledge that and express your gratitude for her. Perhaps you feel like your life has started rolling down a tumultuous road, and she brings you a sense of stability you don't get anywhere else. Tell her how her qualities positively impact you, your life, and your relationship. A simple "thank you" can go a long way.

Make Room for Quality Time

Spend quality time together to explore and appreciate your emotional strengths. Engage in activities that allow you to showcase your respective qualities. For example, CDs can guide deep, meaningful conversations, while MYs can plan exciting, adventurous outings. During this quality time, it may also be important to open up communication about emotions and feelings. Encourage each other to express how you're feeling and why. CDs may prefer in-depth discussions, while MYs might use more expressive and spontaneous forms of communication. Strive for a balance between emotional intensity and stability. Recognize that both intense emotional experiences and calm, grounding moments have their place in a healthy relationship.

Learn from Each Other to Obtain Emotional Growth

Embrace the opportunity to learn from each other's emotional strengths. CDs can learn to embrace spontaneity and adaptability from MYs. Meanwhile, MYs can benefit from the introspection and depth of CDs. Commit to growing emotionally as a couple by lending your emotional strengths to your partner. Explore ways to develop and refine your emotional strengths, both individually and collectively.

Offer Support to MYs in their Social Endeavors

We have spoken about MYs and their social endeavors, but by supporting your MY woman in what she is drawn to, such as her social endeavors, you are strengthening the emotional bond within your relationship. Ways to support and encourage those endeavors include:

- Encouraging her attendance at parties and celebrating her for the social butterfly she is.

- Actively participating in social events and outings with her.

- Respecting her independence and the time she sets aside for friends.

- Planning surprise parties for her.

Understand and Listen to CDs in their Introspective Moments

Understanding CDs during their introspective moments is essential to building a strong and empathetic connection. Here's how to navigate these reflective periods:

- Respect her need for solitude and create a supportive environment for her to be alone.

- Practice patience. Don't rush her into doing things that make her uncomfortable

- Validate her emotions.

- Avoid judgment.

- Respect her privacy.

- Express your availability to talk whenever she is ready

Understanding and listening to your CD wife or girlfriend, especially during times of reflection, shows that you are a supportive and trustworthy partner. In this way, you can build intimacy with her by creating a safe and non-judgmental space for her to flourish.

Recognize and Validate Each Other's Fears and Vulnerabilities

Recognizing and validating each other's fears and vulnerabilities is a crucial aspect of emotional respect in a relationship. Encourage open and honest conversations about your fears and vulnerabilities with her. Create a safe space where both of you feel comfortable sharing these sensitive aspects of yourselves, and when she opens up about her fears and vulnerabilities, practice active listening. Pay close attention to what she is saying and try to understand the emotions behind her words. Avoid interrupting or offering immediate solutions.

Allow for Vulnerability

Being vulnerable in a relationship is essential because genuine emotional connection requires honesty and trust, both of which entail a sense of vulnerability. Opening up and being honest with her requires you to be vulnerable. It takes a lot of trust to be vulnerable with someone, so just by sharing your feelings, she can understand that you are opening up in a way that proves your devotion to her.

In a long-term, committed relationship, you must be willing to show all angles of yourself to engage in full intimacy. The more you can be open and honest about your feelings, the more she can understand you, and the greater the potential for her to feel safe enough to be vulnerable. Especially since if you're comfortable with being vulnerable with her, she'll feel confident that you'll accept when she is vulnerable, too.

Vulnerability can be a struggle, but it truly can help you feel more confident in your relationship if you're able to open up to that level. It not only shows that you love and trust her, but it also reflects courage since divulging ourselves fully to others is one of the scariest situations we can find ourselves in.

Why is that, though? After all, we aren't born afraid of vulnerability. In fact, as infants, we must be vulnerable with our mothers, crying at our every need just to survive. The reasons why we grow afraid are due to:

- Trauma.

- Rejection.

- Cultural/Familial Expectations.

Somewhere along the way, someone has hurt us during a moment of vulnerability. It is important that we do not penalize our current partners for what has happened in the past, no matter how afraid we are. In fact, it is critical that you heal from any fears if you want your relationship to become as intimate as possible. Professional guidance and psychological exercises can help with this tremendously if you feel you are struggling.

Provide Empathy and Understanding

When she decides to be vulnerable with you, ensure you are empathetic and understanding. Remind yourself how difficult it might have been for her to confide in you in this way. Treat this moment for exactly what it is: an incredibly intimate one. Put yourself in her shoes to understand her perspective.

Give Her Complete Validation and Avoid Judgment

When she shares her fears or vulnerabilities, validate her feelings, even if you think it's silly. It's essential to create a judgment-free zone. Let her know that it's okay to feel the way she does and that you understand why she might feel that way. Avoid dismissing her emotions or downplaying her concerns. She trusted you enough to bring these fears to you, so respect them.

Share Your Own Vulnerabilities

Vulnerability begets vulnerability. By sharing your fears and vulnerabilities, you encourage her to do the same. This mutual sharing shows your trust in one another.

Offer Reassurance

Reassure your partner that you are there for her (especially if she's an MY who needs regular affirmations). Tell her that you'll support her in facing her fears or working through her vulnerabilities. Your support can provide her with more comfort than you realize.

Work Together

If she shares fears or vulnerabilities related to a specific area in your relationship, work together to find solutions or strategies to address them. Collaborative problem-solving can even strengthen your connection because it shows that you listened to her feelings and that those feelings were important enough to you that you were willing to do something to change them. Recognizing and validating each other's fears and vulnerabilities can deepen your emotional connection and create a supportive, nurturing environment within your relationship.

Explore A Wide Range of Emotions Together Through Media and Art

Exploring a wide range of emotions together through various forms of media and art can be a meaningful way to connect with your partner on an emotional level and have a little fun in the process.

Choose Emotionally Rich Content

Select books, movies, TV shows, music, or art that delve into complex emotions and themes. Look for content that resonates with both of you and sparks meaningful discussions. Don't limit yourselves. The sky is the limit. There are so many genres to choose from, so there is no reason to select a single one. Explore a variety of genres and styles to experience a broader range of emotions.

Schedule Movie or Reading Nights

Set aside dedicated time for watching movies or reading books together. These shared moments can lead to insightful conversations about the characters' emotions and motivations. You can even create a game where you relate a situation that the characters experienced to your relationship or life in general. This game can lead to a deep conversation that delves into your wife's or girlfriend's psyche, helping you understand each other on a more profound level.

Discuss What You Watch or Read

When you are participating in solo hobbies and happen to watch a movie or read a book that you find particularly interesting, discuss your thoughts and feelings with her. Share how the content made you feel and what aspects of it resonated with you. You can even challenge each other by reading the same book and comparing notes at the end.

Attend Art Exhibitions, Museums, or Cultural Events

The arts are a great outlet for emotions. They can also be a lot of fun and a great date night activity. Visit art exhibitions or museums and explore different forms of visual art with her. Art can evoke powerful emotions and provide a platform for discussing your interpretations and reactions more deeply. Attend cultural events or performances in your community, such as theater productions, concerts, or dance performances. These experiences can enrich your creative mind and mental health and create wonderful bonding experiences with your partner.

Create Art Together

Another excellent bonding experience is creating art together. This collaboration gives you a tangible representation of your relationship. Creating art together can be therapeutic and an expressive way to connect. It allows both of you to bring different talents and perspectives to the table. A work of art created by two different personalities and people can be wild and entertaining to view when completed. Paint a picture together, draw something, or create a sculpture. Whatever you decide, it will be unique and an ultimate showcase of your partnership.

Share Music

Exchange music playlists or songs that hold special meaning for you, especially songs that remind you of her. Music often has the power to evoke deep emotions and memories and is a great way to express something that we can't always express ourselves.

Write Together

Consider writing poetry or stories together. Collaboratively exploring your emotional and creative landscapes can show you a different side of each other that you might not have ever seen before. This is another fun activity that allows both parties to bring something unique to the table and create something that reflects both of your personalities.

Key Takeaways

In this chapter, we journeyed into the realm of emotions. To resonate emotionally with your partner is the ultimate goal in any relationship, and each personality type and individual holds their own unique emotional strengths. Celebrate the diverse emotional landscapes of CDs and MYs. Recognize that both personality types contribute unique strengths and sensitivities to the relationship.

- **Celebrate the Differences Each Partner Brings to the Relationship**: CDs generally provide stability, space, calm clarity, and a shoulder to cry on. While MYs can bring optimism, energy, excitement, cheer, and a hand to hold. Each personality type is different, with its own strengths. Celebrate those, and communicate to your partner all the ways you appreciate them.

- **Always Express Your Gratitude**: Daily life and our hectic schedules can make it hard for us to notice the little things our partners do for us. Notice the ways your woman supports you, from cooking dinner and doing the dishes to picking up your favorite snacks from the store.

- **Offer Support and Understanding**: Drawing on and complementing your partner's strengths with your own makes for a successful relationship with two well-rounded people. But with our strengths come our weaknesses. Balance is key; support your partner on their off days, and they'll do the same for you.

- **Recognize and Validate Her Insecurities**: Just because you think she's amazing doesn't mean she knows that. Don't keep it locked inside. Discuss your fears and insecurities with one another. And make sure you validate them. Be open with one another and express your love and affection every day.

- **Share Your Vulnerabilities**: Learn that it's okay to be vulnerable. Your woman understands you're only human.

She doesn't expect perfection, and admitting your mistakes and fears to her will allow her to know you better and feel more comfortable expressing herself around you.

- **Explore the Power of Art**: Sometimes, talking about our emotions can be difficult. Art, writing, painting, and other crafting are great outlets for our emotions. Take an art class, visit a museum, or enjoy a personal concert together. Talk about the ways you learned and grew from these experiences.

- **Make Magic Together**: Never stop trying to woo your partner. Make her a playlist or poem that expresses how you feel about her. Or share in this creativity together. Collaborate on a painting or a story. Save what you've created and look back on it later. These are great ways to explore your inner selves, spark meaningful conversations, and deepen your connection to each other.

More than anything, ensure that you are open and honest with your woman to the fullest extent. Being vulnerable and resonating with each other on the deepest emotional level possible is critical for a healthy and successful relationship. Besides, she will know you're holding back if you aren't completely open with her. Show her that you love and trust her enough to expose yourself from all angles and rely on each other to fill in the emotional gaps when either of you falls short.

Chapter Six

Maintaining Healthy Finances

Maintaining healthy finances can be a complicated and stressful venture. It doesn't just happen overnight. The key to success lies in patience, understanding, and flexibility. In this chapter, we will delve into the vital role that financial discussions play in your relationship. With 70% of Americans reporting that they feel stressed about money, and many studies showing that economic differences make huge impacts on romantic relationships—usually for the worst—it's crucial that you discuss financial matters with your partner. In fact, studies show that money is one of the most common sources of conflict in marriages. Many even go as far as to claim that it is the second leading cause of divorce.

Financial discussions can cover everything from past mistakes to differing money management philosophies. Set the tone early for your financial goals and communicate your current financial status. Continue reading to learn how to convey your finances with your partner, propose goals, and achieve them so that you can craft a financial plan together. Set yourselves apart from the average couple and ensure that finances don't disrupt your romantic future.

Address Financial Matters with Patience and Understanding

When you find yourself in a long-term, committed relationship, it is vital that you open up the floor to having financial conversations. These conversations may require patience while you communicate to ensure that both of you are on the same page regarding your financial goals and responsibilities. Initiate honest and transparent conversations about your own personal financial situation.

Create a safe space where you and your partner can freely discuss your economic history, current circumstances, and future goals. This dialogue lays the foundation for a deeper understanding of each other's perspectives. Pay close attention to your partner's financial concerns and goals. Encourage her to share her thoughts and feelings about money matters without judgment.

Respect Differences

Recognize that you and your partner may have different financial habits. You may also have different priorities. She may enjoy buying eight-dollar coffees every day, and you may be bothered by that. You may have a mountain of credit card debt, and she may be bothered by that. She may prefer to rent a home rather than buy one, whereas you want to buy a home as soon as you can. You may choose to save all your money while she prefers to save little. Rather than viewing these differences as obstacles, see them as opportunities for compromise and growth. Respect each other's viewpoints and work together to find common ground.

Trust Each Other Financially

As we've learned throughout this book, trust in your relationship is essential. The same can be said for trust in financial matters. Honesty, transparency, and reliability are key components of trust. You create economic trust by consistently working together and respecting each other's financial boundaries.

These financial matters must be addressed with patience and understanding, even if you feel she's misinformed in her goals or perspective. This conversation is a continuous process that contributes to the financial well-being of both partners. It ensures that you are aligned in your financial goals and empowers you to face financial challenges as a united team. It's quite possible that you may choose to keep finances separate after your conversations. In this case, you should make an agreement concerning bills and necessities, especially if you live together or are planning to in the future.

Make a Financial Plan or Goal Together

Setting clear financial goals and creating a plan to achieve them is a powerful way to ensure financial stability and harmony, not just in your relationship but in your life together. Generally, couples can find enough common ground to create financial plans together, but the groundwork needs to be completed first.

Define Your Goals

Start by identifying your shared financial goals. These may include buying a home, saving for your children's education, or achieving financial independence. Understanding your objectives provides clarity and motivation. Discuss your short-term and long-term financial goals as a couple. Whether you're saving for a major purchase, planning for retirement, or aiming to reduce debt, having clear objectives helps you both stay motivated and accountable.

Short-Term vs. Long-Term Plans

Differentiate between your short-term and long-term goals. Short-term goals could involve paying off credit card debt or saving for a vacation, while long-term goals may revolve around retirement planning and wealth accumulation. Make sure you get the complete picture from her and express to her your short-term and long-term plans. Understand that these goals may change and adapt as time goes on.

Prioritize Your Shared Goals

Rank your combined goals based on their importance and urgency. Decide which goals you want to focus on first and allocate resources accordingly. If your credit card debt is unmanageable or you don't have savings, those may be considered great initial priorities.

Allocate Your Budget

If you live together or are hoping to live together in the future, make sure that you review your combined budget and allocate funds to each of your respective goals. Determine how much money you need to set aside regularly to achieve them, but most importantly, be realistic about what you can afford to contribute.

Collaborate on creating a shared budget that reflects your financial goals and individual contributions as well as hers. This budget should encompass all aspects of both of your lives, from daily expenses like that eight-dollar coffee to long-term investments such as a house or retirement.

Set Aside an Emergency Fund

Establishing an emergency fund is a crucial step in financial planning. It would be beneficial to agree on the amount you both feel comfortable saving and prioritize building this fund to provide a safety net for unexpected expenses or emergencies.

Deal with Debt

This should be near the top of your goal list. If either partner has existing debts, it is important to discuss strategies for managing and reducing them. It is recommended that you work together to create a plan that allows you to tackle this debt while maintaining your financial stability. Often, debts like school loans or credit cards have repayment plans. Discuss these monthly payments with your partner, and do the research to see if they can be reduced and how combining finances might affect them.

Review Your Goals Regularly

Periodically review your financial plan together. Finances aren't necessarily the best date night conversation, but you can make this fun. Do it over dinner or coffee at a new place. Assess your progress, make adjustments as needed, and celebrate milestones along the way.

Navigate Familial and External Financial Opinions

In every relationship, external factors can influence financial decisions. Friends, family members, and even the expectations society places on us can play a significant role in how we manage our finances. Part of the discussion you and your partner should have is how much you will allow external factors to impact you. Discuss any family expectations or foreseeable societal pressures with your partner to set up your finances for success.

Set Boundaries and Be a United Front

Establish clear boundaries with external parties regarding your finances. Politely but firmly communicate that your financial decisions are made jointly as a couple and that you appreciate their input but will make choices that align with what you and your partner have decided. Present a united front with this, too, especially if one partner is more easily swayed or pressured by their family or peers.

Maintain Independence and Prioritize Your Relationship

If at all possible, maintain financial freedom and independence from family. Financial freedom can cause strain if your family doesn't see eye to eye with your partner. If either of you depend on your family for financial support, they may feel entitled to have a say in your financial matters. While there are unfortunate moments when you might need help or advice from family or friends, it's crucial to remember the boundaries you have already set with your partner. If you do need help from a family member, discuss how this support might temporarily affect your boundaries. Always prioritize your relationship and your partner's opinion over everyone else's, no matter the circumstance. After all, it's their finances as well.

However, a toxic relationship that lacks trust and respect can lead to financial abuse. If you feel like this may be happening to you, contact a specialist to get help.

Respect Each Type's Financial Priorities and Plan for Future Securities, Such as Investments and Savings

One of the most crucial aspects of financial freedom is planning for your future and having your priorities in check. Ways to navigate this include:

- **Budgeting Together**: Create a budget that reflects your joint financial goals and priorities. Be realistic and flexible, and don't be too harsh on yourselves if you have to adjust as situations arise.

- **Pinpointing Financial Responsibilities**: Clarify each partner's role in managing finances.

- **Emergency Planning**: Discuss and plan for unexpected financial challenges, such as medical expenses or a job loss. How much do you need to set aside? Answer that and make a plan.

- **Investing for the Future**: Explore investment options that align with your long-term financial goals. These investments might include retirement accounts, stocks, bonds, or investing in other avenues. Meet with a financial planner if you need advice on how to reach your goals.

- **Balancing Lifestyle Choices**: Strike a balance between enjoying your present life and saving for the future. It's essential to allocate resources for immediate gratification and long-term security; otherwise, you won't make sustainable progress.

Remember That You Two Are a Team Working Toward a Shared Goal

In the realm of finances, stresses are sure to arise, as are disagreements. Remember that you and your partner are a team. You both contribute to the success of your financial journey together, so it is crucial that you consistently ensure you are on the same page.

During your financial meetings with each other, make sure that you:

- Encourage one another.

- Are completely transparent.

- Are open to changing previously discussed plans.

Life is unpredictable, and there will be bumps in the road and obstacles to navigate. Approach these situations as a team, supporting each other through transitions.

Key Takeaways:

Financial discussions can be challenging, but patience and understanding are key. Always approach financial matters with empathy, acknowledging that each of you may have different attitudes and approaches to your money.

While most couples combine their assets, it is entirely possible to have some separation. Just make sure that both of you are on the same page about what responsibilities the other has. Work together to establish clear financial goals that align with your shared vision.

Try to maintain independence from others, as this can often lead to external opinions being thrust upon you and your partner's finances. Have discussions with your wife or girlfriend about your financial independence from others and set boundaries on what you will and will not allow others to be a part of.

And remember, ultimately, your goals are yours and your partner's alone. While others may have opinions, it is your choice whether or not you listen to or allow them to communicate those opinions. Recognize that the only person you need to satisfy is yourself and your partner. To maintain financial security and alleviate as much stress as possible, make sure you have open communication and regular meetings, and set yourselves up for success in the following ways:

- **Respect Your Differences**: You each had your own lives before coming together in your relationship. Therefore, you may have your own preferences when it comes to spending money. Respect these differences and discuss your goals. Work together to determine areas you would like to compromise or keep finances separate.

- **Have Complete Trust in Your Partner**: Finances are an extension of your relationship. If you trust your partner emotionally and physically, then trust them financially as well. Remember, you are on the same team. If you feel like your concerns aren't being heard or acknowledged, reference previous chapters on how to communicate these worries to your partner effectively.

- **Make a Financial Plan Together**: Keep each of your goals in mind as you discuss and create a financial plan. Listen to your partner and respect what they have to say. Financial discussions can be difficult. Make them more relaxing with calming music, comforting drinks, or games. Remember, it doesn't need to be solved in one conversation. If either of you begins to get frustrated, pause and take a step back.

- **Separate Long-Term Goals and Short-Term Goals**: Decide what goals you want to reach soon and which goals you would like to save for long term. Short-term goals might be saving for furniture, an exciting trip, or paying off manageable debt. Long-term goals might include buying a house, saving for retirement, or putting away money for a wedding or your child's college fund.

- **Create a Budget**: Once you've discussed your goals and understood your and your partner's views on finances, it's time to create a budget. Budgets can be created for monthly expenses and for future planning. If it feels overwhelming, get a professional to help you and your partner come up with a manageable plan.

- **Have an Emergency Fund**: Unfortunately, life does not always go to plan. Emergencies happen. Prepare for them by setting aside money for an emergency fund. Determine how much money you will each add to this fund monthly with your partner.

- **Discuss (Don't Dismiss) Debt**: Debt can be a point of contention in a relationship, but many people carry it with them. Discuss your debt openly with your partner, and allow them to discuss theirs with you. Figure out how you each want to handle your debt and whether it is something you need to solve individually or together.

- **Review Goals Regularly**: As your life together grows, your goals will naturally change. Unexpected surprises may add to or take away from financial stresses. Review your goals, and celebrate the ones you accomplish, like paying off debt or buying a house, together.

Chapter Seven

Cultivate a Lifelong Romance

Cultivating a lifelong romance goes beyond that of personality differences. In this chapter, we will delve into the art of cultivating a lifelong romance and how investing your time and energy can grow your relationship into the real deal: a true love story.

Renew Commitment Vows on Milestone Dates

Commitment is the glue holding your relationship together. Without committing to one another, you would have no relationship. Because of this, it is essential to reaffirm or renew your commitment to one another periodically. Renew your devotion through a vow renewal ceremony. This can be an intimate event or a larger celebration with friends and family. It's a powerful way to reaffirm your love for one another.

Write heartfelt vows that express your love, appreciation, and commitment to her. Be specific about the qualities you cherish most about her. Consider exchanging some kind of token just like you did with your wedding rings on your wedding day. These symbols can be tangible reminders of this renewal, as well as a reminder of your love and dedication to one another.

Even if you aren't married, you can still reaffirm your commitment by sharing vows, celebrating your milestones, taking the next step, or getting engaged. It's okay for your relationship to look different to others; what's most important is to honor your partner and your bond together in the way that best fits your unique relationship and reflects each of your personalities.

Take Time for You and Your Partner to Laugh and Have Fun

If you were asked what first attracted you to her, it likely wouldn't be that she was boring or that she nagged too much. It would likely be "She was funny" or "She had a great sense of humor." So, break up the boring and monotonous day-to-day. Have fun. Laugh together. Frequently, couples allow humor and laughter to drain from the relationship when it shouldn't. A good sense of humor not only brings joy but also alleviates stress.

Have you ever noticed that you feel a bit lighter when you watch one of those silly romantic comedies with her? That's because laughter releases endorphins. So share laughter as often as you can. Just remember to laugh with one another and not at one another.

Share Jokes and Explore Comedy

Cultivate a collection of inside jokes only the two of you understand. These shared moments of humor create a unique bond and keep your connection light-hearted, fun, and engaging. Watch stand-up comedy, funny movies, or even play pranks together. Send each other funny memes, videos, or articles throughout the workday. It's a simple way to brighten each other's day and show her that you're thinking of her.

Be Careful! There's Good Humor and Bad Humor

Facts don't lie. People enjoy laughing. They also enjoy people who enjoy laughing. But be careful with what jokes you tell. Steer away from sensitive topics, and never make fun of your partner. It is also worth noting to steer away from self-deprecating and self-defeating humor, which pokes fun at yourself or pranks that she doesn't find funny.

Set Playful Challenges

To keep the fun alive, consider engaging in friendly competitions or challenges, whether it's a board game, a video game, or a sports activity. Playfulness adds an element of excitement to your relationship. Consider organizing game nights with friends or as a couple. Board games, card games, or even trivia nights offer lots of opportunities for laughter and fun.

Dance Together

Dance in the living room to your favorite songs, even if neither of you is an expert. It's a fantastic way to let loose and share a close, intimate moment. It might sound like a cliche, but it's a go-to move for a reason. Not only can dancing create laughter and fun, but it can also build intimacy.

Explore Local Attractions

Visit local attractions you haven't explored before. Be tourists in your own town, discovering hidden gems and having a blast doing it. Sometimes, we become so complacent in our normal lives that we forget that our backyards often hold a lot of excitement just waiting to be had.

Engage in Romantic Activities Such as Couple Massages or Weekend Getaways

Romantic activities keep the spark alive in your relationship. Spending quality time together is important, and it is equally essential to occasionally pamper yourselves with extra outings or experiences that heighten romantic feelings and emotions.

Get a Couple's Massage

Treat yourselves to a relaxing and intimate couple's massage. It's a great way to unwind, relieve stress, and connect physically and emotionally. Many spas offer packages designed specifically for couples who want to do this activity together.

Plan Weekend Getaways

Plan occasional weekend getaways to escape the routine and monotony of daily life. Explore new places, stay in charming bed and breakfasts, or relax in a cozy cabin in the woods. The change of scenery can reignite your sense of adventure and allow you to see your partner in a new light.

Remember that romantic activities don't have to be extravagant; what matters most is the effort and thought you put into them. Regularly incorporating these types of experiences into your relationship helps maintain the excitement and keeps the connection between you strong. Think of it as being forever-newlyweds.

Don't Be Afraid of Counseling When Needed

Seeking counseling or therapy isn't a sign of weakness but a testament to your commitment to maintaining a healthy and thriving relationship. A skilled therapist can help you and your partner develop more effective communication skills. They can teach you how to express your needs, actively listen, constructively resolve conflicts, and keep feedback neutral. Here's how couples counseling can be beneficial:

- **Communication Improvement**: If effective communication is difficult for the two of you after educating yourselves through this book, it's possible that counseling can help bridge any gaps you might have or help you resolve a long-standing problem.

- **Conflict Resolution**: If you can't seem to find common ground during your discussions or feel that your check-ins are often more negative than positive, bringing in a neutral party can help you find solutions you may not have considered.

- **Reigniting Intimacy**: If you feel as though the flame is dying out in terms of physical touch or emotional intimacy, a sex therapist might help you reignite that spark.

- **Navigating Life's Changes**: Major life transitions will occur as you journey through life with your woman. Parenthood, career changes, and illnesses can strain relationships and leave you in doubt. Navigating these with professionals can be beneficial if there seems to be a disconnect during these transitional moments.

- **Learning Healthy Patterns**: As you become further ingrained in your habits, it is often easy to unknowingly repeat unhealthy ones. Therapy can help the two of you recognize and change these unhealthy patterns.

Remember that counseling doesn't imply that your relationship is in crisis. It can be a proactive step to enhance your connection, deepen your understanding of each other, and ensure a fulfilling and loving partnership. Use your therapist as a tool to improve your relationship. After all, we want to be the best version of ourselves independently of our partners; why not be the best version of ourselves alongside our partners? If you're considering counseling, look for a licensed therapist or counselor specializing in couples or relationship therapy.

Experience New Activities, Hobbies, or Restaurants Together

Our journey through life is all about exploration. Exploring with your woman is key to keeping your spark alive. Exploring new experiences together can infuse excitement and novelty into your relationship like nothing else quite can. Do you remember the first time you tried doing a hobby you loved? Of course, you do! Imagine if every new thing you tried from here on out was with your wife or girlfriend. Wouldn't that permanently place her in many positive memories?

Discovering and trying new things together is a chance to bond over shared interests and passions, whether you know you have them or not. More than that, though, discovering new things is the only thing that breaks up the monotonous and mundane. The key to keeping her interested is for you to be interested, and what better way than to inject a bit of freshness into your lives?

When exploring new activities, consider her interests and preferences. You can take turns choosing activities with her, ensuring you both have a say. Be open to trying things you may not have considered before; you might come to find that you enjoy something you never thought you could.

Whether trying a new cuisine, taking up a dance class, embarking on a road trip, or learning a new skill, the key is approaching these experiences with an open heart and a willingness to embrace the unknown. Know that at the end of the day, even if you don't enjoy the activity, you're doing something different with your wife or girlfriend. These shared adventures will keep your relationship fresh and exciting and provide opportunities for growth and connection.

Remember that CDs and MYs may enjoy different activities, but it's important for you both to try new things even if you don't think you'll love them. You might surprise yourselves! To make this a part of your regular scheduled dates, consider being the first to suggest it. Start with something you know she will enjoy doing to get the ball rolling!

If you want to experience a new activity with your CD partner, you could try:

- Starting a book club for two.
- Stretching it out with some yoga at a studio or at home.
- Playing games or doing puzzles together.
- Gardening together.
- Starting a collection.
- Beer brewing at home.
- Learning how to knit together.

Activities you may want to try with your MY partner include:

- Trying your hand at tie-dying.
- Learning a new language together.
- Cooking together.
- Going to an unknown band's concert.
- Trying a martial arts class.
- Going camping or biking.

- Rock climbing.

- Volunteering at a local soup kitchen.

Share and Support Each Other's Dreams and Aspirations

In a healthy and thriving relationship, partners support each other's dreams and aspirations. Sharing and supporting each other's dreams and aspirations:

- Builds trust.

- Promotes teamwork.

- Provides motivation.

- Leads to emotional fulfillment.

When you support your partner's dreams, you demonstrate trust and faith in their abilities. This trust is the bedrock of a strong and lasting partnership. Sharing your dreams and aspirations with your partner fosters a deeper emotional connection. It allows you to understand each other on a profound level. Encouraging each other's goals promotes a sense of teamwork. You become each other's biggest cheerleaders, working together to achieve individual and shared dreams. Knowing that your partner believes in your dreams can be incredibly motivating. Their support can give you the confidence to pursue your goals.

Achieving your dreams can lead to personal fulfillment and happiness. Your partner's support in this journey can contribute to your overall well-being. Remember that supporting each other's dreams doesn't mean sacrificing your own. It's about finding a balance where both partners can pursue their aspirations while nurturing the relationship. A supportive and nurturing partnership can provide the stability and encouragement needed to reach for the stars.

Respect and Encourage Each Other's Personal Development

In a lasting and thriving relationship, personal growth and development should be celebrated and encouraged. Respecting and encouraging her personal development allows for her individual fulfillment and trust.

Personal growth leads to a sense of fulfillment and self-actualization. Encouraging her development means you're both on a journey toward becoming the best versions of yourselves. When both partners are committed to personal growth, it can strengthen their emotional bond. The general hope of being in a long-term relationship is to grow old together. This means growing together emotionally, mentally, and spiritually. To do this, it's essential that you learn from one another and become more connected in your journey together.

By supporting each other's personal development, you create a supportive environment where both partners can explore new interests and passions and grow individually. Embracing personal growth means you're open to change and adaptation for yourself and for your relationship. This growth can be invaluable when facing life and everything that comes with it. As two people grow and evolve, the relationship can also grow and evolve.

The best ways to respect and encourage each other as you move toward your personal development are included below:

- Celebrating the progress that she has made

- Providing space for personal reflection

- Giving her insight by sharing what you have learned about her along the way

- Being open to change

- Encouraging self-care

Allow each other the space and time needed for personal growth. Sometimes, personal development requires solitary activities or self-reflection. When you come back together or during your regular check-ins, share what you've learned from these journeys. It can spark interesting conversations, and you may find that you begin to inspire each other.

Revisit Places of Mutual Significance

Revisiting places that are important to you is often an emotional experience, but revisiting a place that is important to both you and your partner is the best medicine for recovering from relationship woes, blues, or just a plain old rut you've found yourselves in. Revisiting places with special meaning for both partners will often rekindle fond memories. Returning to places where you've shared significant moments can evoke nostalgia and remind you of the journey you've taken together. It may even remind you why you fell in love in the first place.

These places are part of your shared life together, and revisiting them reinforces the idea that you've built something meaningful over time. Reliving positive experiences can benefit both of you and your respective mental health. Make the most out of revisiting these locations in the following ways:

- **Plan Together**: Discuss which places hold the most meaning for each of you. It could be where you had your first date, got engaged, or even just somewhere you had a particularly memorable date.

- **Schedule Visits:** Make plans to visit these places periodically. You can schedule a day trip or weekend getaway to spend quality time there. Definitely consider making these revisits part of an anniversary tradition or ritual.

- **Create New Memories:** Don't always rely on your nostalgia to get you through the trip. When you return to this special place, make sure you're trying to create new memories together.

- **Share Reflections:** Talk about your feelings and memories associated with these places. This is a great bonding exercise to promote intimacy.

- **Stay Present:** While revisiting, stay present in the moment. Put away your cell phone and focus on only her.

Celebrate Anniversaries with Unique Traditions

Anniversaries are significant milestones in any relationship. They mark another year of love, growth, and commitment. To keep your love thriving, consider celebrating your anniversaries with unique traditions that are meaningful to both of you.

Develop Personal Rituals

Create personal anniversary rituals that reflect your love story. It could be as simple as watching the sunrise together on the morning of your anniversary, preparing a special breakfast, or revisiting the place where you first met. Make a ritual or tradition a part of your anniversary celebration.

Write Love Letters

Exchange heartfelt love letters on your anniversary. Express your feelings, share your hopes and dreams, and reflect on your time together. These letters will become cherished mementos of your history, past, and future. Save them, and pull them out to read them on big milestone anniversaries to reflect on your time together.

Make a Memory Book/Box

Start a memory book or scrapbook, or make a box dedicated to your relationship. Add mementos such as ticket stubs to concerts or shows, photos, and notes. It's a tangible reminder of your shared experiences. Add to it on your anniversary with whatever you decide to do to celebrate. If you go out for a night on the town, take a photograph and add it to your collection. If you go to a show, keep the ticket. When you add a new item, take the time to look through what you've already collected. Enjoy the memories these mementos bring up, and share those stories with your loved one.

Renew Your Vows

As mentioned earlier, periodically renewing your commitment is important. Consider renewing your commitment vows on milestone anniversaries. Whether it's a private ceremony or a gathering with friends and family, reaffirming your love can be a deeply meaningful experience and a way to add to and refresh vows you may have made a long time ago. Now that you have grown together in your relationship and as individuals, you may have a little more wisdom to add to those initial vows.

Give Gifts with Meaning

Instead of extravagant gifts, you could shake things up and make a tradition of giving sentimental gifts instead. It could be a piece of jewelry you made, a hand-crafted card, or something that symbolizes your journey together. Consider exchanging these types of gifts as part of a tradition for your anniversary and other milestone celebrations.

Practice Acts of Service

On your anniversary, take your love for one another and share it with the world. For example, you could spend your anniversary serving others in the community. Of course, you can also serve your wife or girlfriend by cooking her a special meal, taking care of extra chores, or planning a special date night, but creating a tradition of giving back might be a unique way to make your anniversaries truly special.

Create and Maintain Relationship Rituals and Promises

Relationships thrive on routines and rituals that reinforce your bond and create a sense of togetherness. These relationship rituals can be simple yet powerful ways to nurture your love and remind your partner that you're thinking of them, even when life gets hectic and stressful.

Make Her Morning Toast

Start each day with a special morning ritual. It could be making her coffee every morning, or it could be taking a morning walk, or sitting at the breakfast table together. It could even just be cuddling for a quick moment before getting up to start your day. These moments set the day off on the right foot for you and your relationship.

Plan a Weekly Date Night

Dedicate a specific night of the week as your date night. Whether you go out for dinner, have a movie night at home, or engage in a shared hobby, this regular date night gives you something to look forward to. It ensures that you both take the time to appreciate one another and continue to foster your bond.

Commit to Daily Check-Ins

Set aside time each day for a brief check-in with your partner. These should be separate from your regular check-ins, as these daily ones should happen more frequently. Share highlights and challenges from your day, or simply ask how she's feeling.

Set Aside Tech-Free Time

Creating tech-free zones or times in your home is a great way to ensure that your partner has your undivided attention. These areas or times are moments in which you can focus solely on each other. Putting away your devices and engaging in meaningful conversation or activities without distractions is intentional quality time. Talk about your day, read together, or engage in a craft. Even washing dishes after dinner can be your tech-free time as long as you spend your time together away from your phones or other technology.

Key Takeaways

In this chapter, we focused on the importance of nurturing and sustaining a deep, lasting romance for years to come. When you wish to cultivate a lifelong romance with your woman, investing daily time and energy is important. Prevent burnout by keeping communication lines open and relying on each other when planning dates or activities so that one partner isn't saddled with all the responsibility. Ultimately, both of you are responsible for fostering a lasting relationship. Some key things to remember when breathing fresh romance back into your relationship and also keeping it there:

- **Embrace Joy and Laughter**: Make time for fun and laughter in your relationship. Engage in activities that bring joy and light-heartedness into both of your lives.

- **Engage in Romantic Activities**: Keep the romance alive with gestures like couple massages and weekend getaways.

If the budget is tight that month, try giving each other massages, turning your bathroom into a spa for two, or having a picnic in your living room.

- **Explore New Experiences:** Continually explore new activities, hobbies, or restaurants together. This keeps your relationship fresh and allows you and your partner to make new memories.

- **Support Each Other's Dreams:** Encourage and actively support each other's individual dreams and aspirations. Your partnership should be a source of inspiration. You both rely on one another's support. Make sure you give it!

- **Respect Personal Development:** Respect each other's personal development journeys. Allow room for self-reflection and solitude if the occasion is needed.

- **Revisit Meaningful Places:** Revisit locations that hold special significance in your relationship. Make the visit worthwhile by creating new memories and expressing your affection during the trip with zero interruptions or distractions.

- **Renew Commitment Vows:** Celebrate your commitment to each other and renew your vows. This is especially a good idea for milestone anniversaries.

- **Celebrate Anniversaries:** Whether you renew your vows on your anniversary or not, make sure you always celebrate it together. Adding in fun and unique traditions also adds some spice to the day. Try to incorporate small or large traditions and keep mementos of the day to look back on later.

Remember, no one wants to see your relationship succeed more than you and your partner. Rely on each other and focus on what's important. Don't hesitate to seek professional guidance if your relationship faces challenges you aren't sure you can overcome on your own. Counseling can provide valuable tools for overcoming obstacles and help you grow together as a couple in a healthy way. If you want a lasting relationship but feel your romance is dwindling, consider a counselor to help the two of you get back on track.

Chapter Eight

Final Thoughts

As we come to the final chapter in this journey on *50 Ways to Love Your Woman*, it's essential to reflect back on the path we've traveled, exploring the intricate dance of love with its different personality types—the Cave Dweller (CD), the Mountain Yeller (MY), and the Straddler, who possesses elements of both. Throughout this book, we have delved into the significance of understanding these personality types, how to communicate effectively with each of them, enhancing physical and emotional intimacy, balancing social lives between differing personalities, resonating emotionally with your partner, maintaining healthy finances, and cultivating a lifelong romance.

Love is truly a dynamic and evolving force that connects us in ways we can never truly predict. Your wife or girlfriend is a human being, and that human being is complex and beautiful. Formulating and fostering a successful romantic relationship is not about finding the perfect formula or mastering a set of guidelines. Instead, it's about the dedication and effort we put into nurturing the unique love we share with our partners. Your wife or girlfriend (whether a CD or an MY or somewhere in between) will appreciate the steps you have taken to communicate with and understand her in a way no one else does. She will appreciate you putting your relationship first and making her a priority.

The Importance of Continuous Effort and Growth in Relationships

Your journey in this book has underscored the importance of continuous effort and growth in relationships. Love is not a static concept but a force that thrives on the energy we invest in it. Every day, we have the opportunity to learn, adapt, and grow in our relationships. Our personalities evolve, and our needs change. It is forever important that we communicate with one another, focus on ourselves and our significant others, and continue to maintain self-growth and growth within our relationships in order to be our happiest selves.

Embrace the Dynamic Nature of Love

Love is not a one-size-fits-all concept. It is as diverse and complex as the human beings who experience it. Through the pages of this book, we've explored the different personalities that you and the women in your life fit into. The fact that each personality type or individual may demonstrate their love differently shows that there is no right or wrong way to love. We must celebrate these differences and embrace the individuality of each and every person and relationship. By acknowledging how we all show and receive affection, we open ourselves up to give love and accept love in deeply profound ways.

Learn Through Differences

The differences between personality types and individuals create an opportunity to truly develop patience, understanding, and empathy, especially when we focus on each other's emotional strengths. In reading *50 Ways to Love Your Woman*, you have expanded your horizon, broadened your perspective, and hopefully received the tools and resources needed to learn from your wife or girlfriend and the love she shares with you. Embrace the differences you offer and accept her unique emotional strengths. Learn from them and enhance your own emotional abilities.

Cherish Your Love

As we conclude this book, it is important for you to leave with the encouragement to continually evolve, adapt, and cherish the love you share with your woman. Use the knowledge and insights gained from this guide as tools to strengthen the bond you have with her.

It is pretty easy to begin to take your wife or girlfriend for granted, especially after growing comfortable with her. Over time, it is natural to stop saying "thank you" as often or to stop pursuing her. This leads to a decline in valuing one another. Which ultimately results in you no longer cherishing one another.

Never stop adoring her. If you can, pretend every day is a new day to find a way to woo her. Use the guidelines of this book to understand her needs and desires and how to continue to make her fall for you each day.

Stay Curious

Curiosity doesn't kill the cat—not in love, that is. It keeps the cat interested and the world around it interesting. Stay curious about yourself and the woman you love, and you'll never become bored or complacent.

Start with yourself. Never stop learning about and working on yourself. It's easy to focus on her shortcomings and overlook your own personal struggles. Hopefully, this book has taught you more about your own motivations, areas of strength and struggle, and any unmet desires or needs that you may have. As you've read, you have developed a new curiosity to discover more about yourself as well as improve on any shortcomings you may have.

When you place your woman on equal footing to your own, you begin to realize it is quite natural to have shortcomings. However, after reflecting on this book, it is also a joy to discover that she also has strengths in areas that you may not have realized, and even if she seems different than she was when you first got together, she still has a lot to offer.

See yourself. See each other. Explore one another and meet in a moment of mutual discovery to grow your intimacy and form a stronger bond with one another. Since neither of you should ever stop growing, there should always be something new to learn about your partner.

Make Time

Of course, curiosity and discovery will take quite a bit of time and investment in your relationship. So, take the time! There will be inconsistency as you both continue your journey together. This inconsistency happens for many different reasons, but mostly when you transition into new seasons of life. These are times of so much chaos and so much change that it's easy to feel spread thin. Prioritize your relationship with her. This is why your regular check-ins are so important. Ask one another, "Are we making enough time for each other? When is the last time we've truly felt like we've been able to go on a date or be alone with one another?" It may seem obvious, but that small gesture will open you both up to being honest about whether you feel properly invested in by your partner.

There are moments when you need to talk about your relationship "business," but also times when one of you just needs to vent or receive emotional support. Remember, you are going through this life *with* her. Make the time to ensure that it's a pleasurable and fulfilling life you two create together. Moments of laughter and silliness or shared activity can bring about a beautiful bond of intimacy at the end of the day. Whether she's a CD, an MY, or somewhere in between, she, like you, craves that precious quality time together. So always make the time. Love, at its core, is all about being present in the moments you share. Make the memories, cherish each other, and embrace the ever-evolving journey of love.

Appendices

Self-Assessment Questionnaire: Determine if You're a CD, MY, or Straddler

In the quest for self-understanding, recognizing one's intrinsic personality traits plays a crucial role. This self-assessment questionnaire has been carefully designed to help you discern whether you align most closely with the introspective nature of a Cave Dweller (CD), the extroverted inclinations of a Mountain Yeller (MY), or the balanced characteristics of a Straddler. By reflecting on your behaviors, preferences, and reactions in various situations, this tool aims to provide insight into your predominant personality type. Approach each question with honesty and openness, and remember, there's no right or wrong answer—just a deeper understanding of your unique self waiting to be unveiled.

Personality Indicator #1

Circle one answer per question.

1. Have you ever walked in your sleep during your adult life?

   YES or NO

2. As a teenager, did you feel comfortable expressing your feelings to one or both of your parents?

   YES or NO

3. Do you have a tendency to look directly into a person's eyes when talking to them?

   YES or NO

4. Do you feel that most people, when you first meet them, are uncritical of your appearance?

   YES or NO

5. In a group situation with people you've just met, would you feel comfortable drawing attention to yourself by initiating a conversation?

   YES or NO

6. Do you feel comfortable holding hands or hugging someone you're in a relationship with in front of other people?

   YES or NO

7. When someone talks about feeling warm physically, do you begin to feel warm also?

YES or NO

8. Do you tend to tune out when someone is talking to you because you're anxious to come up with your side of the story?

YES or NO

9. Do you feel that you learn better by seeing and/or reading than by hearing?

YES or NO

10. In a new class or company meeting, do you usually feel comfortable asking questions in front of the group?

YES or NO

11. When expressing your ideas, do you find it important to relate all the details leading up to the subject so the other person can understand it completely?

YES or NO

12. Do you enjoy relating to children?

YES or NO

13. Are you comfortable with your body movements when faced with unfamiliar people and circumstances?

YES or NO

14. Do you prefer reading fiction rather than non-fiction?

    YES or NO

15. If you were to imagine sucking on a juicy lemon, would your mouth water?

    YES or NO

16. Do you feel comfortable receiving a compliment in front of other people?

    YES or NO

17. Do you feel that you're a good conversationalist?

    YES or NO

18. Do you feel comfortable when complimentary attention is drawn to your physical body?

    YES or NO

Personality Indicator # 2

Circle one answer per question.

1. Have you ever awakened in the middle of the night and felt that you could not move your body and/or talk?

    YES or NO

2. As a child, did you feel you were more affected by your parents' tone of voice than by what they actually said?

YES or NO

3. If someone you know talks about a fear that you've experienced before, do you have a tendency to re-experience that apprehension or fear?

YES or NO

4. After having an argument with someone, do you tend to dwell on what you could or should have said?

YES or NO

5. Do you tend to occasionally tune out when someone is talking to you and therefore don't hear what's being said because your mind drifts to something totally unrelated?

YES or NO

6. Do you sometimes desire to be complimented for a job well done, but feel embarrassed or uncomfortable when complemented?

YES or NO

7. Do you often fear not being able to carry on a conversation with someone you've just met?

YES or NO

8. Do you feel self-conscious when attention is drawn to your

physical body or appearance?

YES or NO

9. If you had a choice, would you rather avoid being around children most of the time?

YES or NO

10. Do you feel uptight in body movements, especially when faced with unfamiliar people or circumstances?

YES or NO

11. Do you prefer reading non-fiction rather than fiction?

YES or NO

12. If someone describes a very bitter taste, do you have difficulty experiencing the physical feeling of that bitter taste?

YES or NO

13. Do you generally feel that you see yourself less favorably than others see you?

YES or NO

14. Do you tend to feel awkward or self-conscious holding hands and/or kissing someone you're in a relationship with, in front of other people?

YES or NO

15. In a new lecture or company meeting, do you usually feel uncomfortable asking questions in front of the group?

    YES or NO

16. Do you feel uneasy if someone you've just met looks you directly in the eyes when talking to you, especially if the conversation is about you?

    YES or NO

17. In a group situation with people you've just met, would you feel uncomfortable drawing attention to yourself by initiating a conversation?

    YES or NO

18. If you're in a relationship or are very close to someone, do you find it difficult or embarrassing to verbalize your love for them?

    YES or NO

Personality Indicator Scores

Personality Indicator #1

- Give yourself 10 points for every yes answer for questions one and two.

- Give yourself 5 points for every YES answer for questions three through eighteen.

- Write the total number at the top of #1's questionnaire.

Personality Indicator #2

- Give yourself 10 points for every yes answer for questions one and two.

- Give yourself 5 points for every YES answer for questions three through eighteen.

- Write the total number at the top of #2's questionnaire.

- Combine the total from PI 1 & 2.

Using the Scoring Chart

On the scoring chart, look up the combined score of Personality Indicators 1 & 2 on the HORIZONTAL axis of the chart and circle the number.

- Take the total score of PI #1, locate it on the VERTICAL axis of the chart, and circle the number.

- Draw a horizontal line across the page from the PI 1 score, then draw a vertical line down from the combined score.

- The number in the box where the two lines intersect represents your true, adjusted percentage personality indicator.

- Scores 61 and higher indicate a Mountain Yeller personality type.

- Scores 45 and lower indicate a Cave Dweller personality type.

- Scores 47 to 56 indicate a Straddler personality type.

Cave Dweller Tendencies

- Reserved
- Head ruled
- Controlling
- Wants space and security
- Prefers socializing one-on-one
- Singular focus
- Thinks before reacting
- Prefers showing affection privately
- Distrusts flattery
- Enjoys working alone
- Enjoys individual activities
- Wants alone time
- Dresses for comfort
- Decides after thinking about it
- Speaks literally, to the point
- Infers from what others say
- Feels emotional pain in the mind

- Fears loss of security

Cave Dweller Priorities

- Career/Financial Security
- Hobbies/Children
- Relationships/Family
- Sex/Lovers

Mountain Yeller Tendencies

- Outgoing
- Heart ruled
- Dominating
- Wants connection and touch
- Enjoys socializing in groups
- Movement focused
- Reacts spontaneously
- Comfortable with affection anytime
- Likes reassurance and compliments
- Enjoys working with people
- Enjoys team activities

- Wants to be together as much as possible
- Decides in the moment
- Speaks inferentially—adds story
- Takes literally what others say
- Feels emotional pain in body and mind
- Fears rejection

Mountain Yeller Priorities

- Relationships/Sex
- Family/Children
- Friends/Hobbies
- Career/Financial security

COMBINED SCORE #1 AND #2

SCORE #1	50	55	60	65	70	75	80	85	90	95	100	105	110	115	120	125	130	135	140	145	150	155	160	165	170	175	180	185	190	195	200
100											100	96	91	87	83	80	77	74	71	69	67	65	61	59	57	56	54	53	51	50	
95										100	95	90	86	83	79	76	73	70	68	66	63	61	59	58	56	54	53	51	50	49	48
90									100	95	90	86	82	78	75	72	69	67	64	62	60	58	56	55	53	51	50	49	47	46	45
85								100	94	89	85	81	77	74	71	68	65	63	61	59	57	55	53	52	50	49	47	46	45	44	43
80							100	94	89	84	80	76	73	70	67	64	62	59	57	55	53	52	50	48	47	46	44	43	42	41	40
75						100	94	88	83	79	75	71	68	65	63	60	58	56	54	52	50	48	47	45	44	43	42	41	39	38	38
70					100	93	88	82	78	74	70	67	64	61	58	56	54	52	50	48	47	45	44	42	41	40	39	38	37	36	35
65				100	93	87	81	76	72	68	65	62	59	57	54	52	50	48	46	45	43	42	41	39	38	37	36	35	34	33	33
60			100	92	86	80	75	71	67	63	60	57	55	52	50	48	46	44	43	41	40	39	38	36	35	34	33	32	32	31	30
55		100	92	85	79	73	69	65	61	58	55	52	50	48	46	44	42	41	39	38	37	35	34	33	32	31	31	30	29	28	28
50	100	91	83	77	71	67	63	59	56	53	50	48	45	43	42	40	39	37	36	34	33	32	31	30	29	29	28	27	26	26	25
45	90	82	75	69	64	60	56	53	50	47	45	43	41	39	38	36	35	33	32	31	30	29	28	27	26	26	25	24	24	23	23
40	80	73	67	62	57	53	50	47	44	42	40	38	36	35	33	32	31	30	29	28	27	26	25	24	24	23	22	22	21	21	20
35	70	64	58	54	50	47	44	41	39	37	35	33	32	30	29	28	27	26	25	24	23	23	22	21	21	20	19	19	18	18	18
30	60	55	50	46	43	40	38	36	33	32	30	29	27	26	25	24	23	22	21	21	20	19	19	18	17	17	16	16	15	15	15
25	50	45	42	38	36	33	31	29	28	26	25	24	23	22	21	20	19	19	18	17	17	16	15	15	14	14	14	13	13	13	12
20	40	36	33	31	29	27	25	24	22	21	20	19	18	17	17	16	15	15	14	14	13	13	13	12	12	11	11	11	11	10	10
15	30	27	25	23	21	20	19	18	17	16	15	14	13	13	12	12	11	11	10	10	10	9	9	9	9	8	8	8	8	8	8
10	20	18	17	15	14	13	13	12	11	11	10	10	9	9	8	8	7	7	7	7	6	6	6	6	6	6	5	5	5	5	5
5	10	9	8	8	7	7	6	6	6	5	5	5	4	4	4	4	4	3	3	3	3	3	3	3	3	3	3	3	3	3	3
0	0	0	0	0	0	0	0	0	0	0	0	0	0	0	0	0	0	0	0	0	0	0	0	0	0	0	0	0	0	0	0

About the Author

Dr. Cline lives with her husband, two daughters, two German Shepherds, and two Yorkies in the hills of North Carolina. Her expertise in relationship building has offered her the opportunity to travel around the world as a keynote speaker and international workshop facilitator.

www.ingramcontent.com/pod-product-compliance
Lightning Source LLC
Chambersburg PA
CBHW071641080526
44586CB00013BA/1213